Gardens
of Philosophy

FICINO ON PLATO

ARTHUR FARNDELL

SHEPHEARD-WALWYN (PUBLISHERS) LTD

First published in 2006 by
Shepheard-Walwyn (Publishers) Ltd
Suite 604, The Chandlery
50 Westminster Bridge Road
London SE1 7QY

British Library Cataloguing in Publication Data
A catalogue record of this book
is available from the British Library

ISBN-13: 978-0-85683-240-6
ISBN-10: 0-85683-240-5 *pub say use this*

Typeset by Alacrity,
Banwell Castle, Weston-super-Mare
Printed through Print Solutions, Wallington, Surrey

CONTENTS

"Epitomes" "Arguments"

Where is the genealogical table?

CONTENTS

Called "Argumenta" in OP?

So why call these Letters of Plato?

to Nic Valori

PREFACE

P LATO HAS EXERTED a major influence on Western civilisation
for nearly two and a half millennia. He and his master Socrates
were chiefly concerned with what constitutes the real happiness
for human beings and with the communication of this to others. For
them, the Good did not consist in wealth, power and the gratification
of the senses, but in the knowledge of the very principle of goodness of
which all those things that seem good are merely transitory reflections.
In Plato's view, the path to the Good lies in the contemplation of the Good
and the practice of the virtues: wisdom, courage, justice, and temperance.

Marsilio Ficino, a Florentine priest of the fifteenth century, was the
last of a long line of philosophers to re-introduce Plato's teaching
into society as a living commitment rather than an abstract theory.
In addition to writing books to show that the works of Plato were in
perfect harmony with the Christian religion, Ficino translated all the
works of Plato from Greek into Latin. He also wrote illuminating
commentaries on Plato's dialogues.

This volume consists of Ficino's shorter commentaries or summaries. They all have as their focus Plato's primary concern with the
Good but the treatment of the theme is refreshingly varied. Neither
Plato nor Ficino was an ivory-tower philosopher: they both believed
that the virtues found within could be practised in the government of
the State. The qualities of the good householder are also the qualities
of the good ruler writ large. In these commentaries the reader will find
an insight into the text of Plato's dialogues which leads to a much
greater understanding of the original master.

No one is better equipped than Arthur Farndell to translate these commentaries. He has a comprehensive knowledge of the Latin language
and a thorough knowledge not only of Plato but also of Ficino, since
he has worked continuously on the translation of Ficino's letters from
Latin into English, of which seven volumes have now been published.

Clement Salaman

Editor of *The Letters of Marsilio Ficino*, Volumes 1-7, published by Shepheard-Walwyn, 1975-2003

THE HISTORICAL CONTEXT

SO MUCH has been written about 'The Renaissance' that some of us may wish that the term – like 'Modern Art' – had never been invented. For instance, some writers have seen the 'Renaissance' as merely an exercise in undue power, wealth, and patronage; some, as the beginning of the creeping worship of consumer goods.

Some trace the phenomenon back to the twelfth century – or even earlier, say the ninth century – which makes it more of a wave-pattern of highs and lows in general human consciousness, stirred by tiny schools of learning: in short, such a shapeless thing in total as almost to be a non-event.

Meanwhile, historians condensing the story of mankind have sought one-liners for this elusive period of history. 'The re-awakening of learning' is a standard one, coined long ago, which neatly allows for a series of foothills before the great mountain of achievement.

However, a few facts or events seem indisputable. Around 1350 there were the stirrings of a new burst of self-awareness, of creative energy, in European mankind. As Latin declined as the common tongue, national and regional tongues became the instruments of higher thought, finding expression through Petrarch, Chaucer, and the mystics of all nations. The Tuscan-speaking 'republic' and/or benign autocracy of free-thinking Florence became a suitable seed-bed for this flowering.

Meanwhile, scholars in Greece and Italy foresaw that the ancient heritage of Greece and Byzantium was under threat: a fate which was to come about in 1453 with the fall of Constantinople and especially the destruction of its precious libraries. Two years later, Athens itself fell to the Turks.

As the common language – the internet – of European scholars was still Latin, this potential treasure trove of gathered knowledge in Greek (then being shipped out of Constantinople in boatloads) required either that scholars, mostly seniors or of middle age, must attempt to learn Greek or that translators with some considerable qualities of intellect and devotion were needed to render this wealth of Greek thought into Latin.

At the top of this list for translation were the works of Plato, the epicentre of Greek thought, along with Aristotle, whose surviving works had by good fortune been preserved in Arabic translation.

Happily, Cosimo de' Medici, who from his youth had been aware of these great movements of human development, found a promising young man, the son of his personal physician, who might be taught Greek and trained to render these works of Plato – which were barely surviving or known in Europe – into Latin.

And so Marsilio Ficino (1433-99) steps onto the stage of history.

Ficino toiled at the translations of Plato's Dialogues from Greek into Latin, just in time to present ten of them to his patron, Cosimo de' Medici, before the latter's death in 1464. The remaining work took a further three years to complete.

Then Ficino, as part of the huge output of his life, provided commentaries to help the understanding of these – effectively brand-new – monuments of thought. And from the intimate acquaintance which a translator acquires with his source and subject, Ficino began to explain Plato's Dialogues to his eminent scholar-friends, and later to kings, rulers, churchmen, and young scholars throughout Europe whom he never met in person, in eloquent letters galloped across mountain and plain.

So this first translation into English by Arthur Farndell of the shorter commentaries by Ficino on the content of Plato's Dialogues, along with Ficino's commentary on the Letters attributed to Plato, mirrors in a further language, English, this same great – truly great – event in the advance of human self-knowledge.

It is suggested that, in order to sustain and advance your interest, you have a translation of Plato's Dialogues to hand, so as to be fully present, so to speak, at this meeting of great minds.

Readers might also like to hold in their imagination, while reading these documents of human thought, this great romance of history: that these are 'seeds of the mind' which were to be scattered across, not merely Europe, but all the world, as Ficino's Latin translations of Plato's Dialogues, along with his own commentaries, spread amongst scholars, later influencing poets such as Spenser and possibly Shakespeare.

How exquisite in its timing, we can now see, was Ficino's lifetime and his vast work, coming as it did in the few years between the development of printing and the discovery of a brave New World which was ultimately to found a new republic based on these very principles and ideals of goodness, truth, and beauty, law and love, liberty, equality and fraternity, the many in the one and the one in the many, the trust in God, which Socrates and Plato together enunciated for us.

Michael Shepherd

Editor of *Friend to Mankind: Marsilio Ficino 1433-1499*, published by Shepheard-Walwyn, 1999

TRANSLATOR'S INTRODUCTION

As a student and young teacher, I found it difficult to get on with Plato and Socrates. They seemed to ask too many questions and to hold the answers (if they had any) close to their chests. They would lead you along a labyrinthine path and then suddenly vanish, leaving you without directions as to how to proceed. Their ways of reasoning seemed arid and barren. Worst of all, they appeared to enjoy making fun of other people's ignorance.

My youthful views underwent a sea-change when I heard someone I greatly respect describe Plato as the Teacher of the West. What a provocative appellation! At that moment was born the resolution to read the whole of Plato's works, with the aim of testing the validity of such a glorious title. It was a resolution that took immediate effect and worked its way into the interstices of daily living, so that, in addition to lengthier periods of reading, Plato's words were being absorbed on London tube trains and whenever I had ten minutes 'free'.

The experience? That of taxiing along the runway for an inordinate length of time, before being unexpectedly whooshed up to the stratosphere; of being charmed by the occasional idyllic scene or the slash of razor-sharp wit; and of being awed by effusions of pure wisdom. The verdict? The provocative appellation merited serious consideration. The result? Love and respect for Socrates and Plato.

When a growing acquaintance with Marsilio Ficino's works, written more than seventeen centuries after the time of Plato, showed that the Florentine philosopher viewed Plato as his teacher, the natural step was a desire to share some of what Ficino says about Platonic philosophy with others who are more at home with English than with Latin. Encouragement from good friends set the translation process in motion some six years ago, and the result is the present volume.

Arthur Farndell

note doesn't mention Valerie Rees

ACKNOWLEDGEMENTS

LOVING THANKS go first and foremost to my wife, Phyllis, who has supported this undertaking from the beginning by reading these translations to me and pointing out with unerring insight all those passages which needed to be re-investigated because they jarred on her sensibilities.

Unreserved gratitude goes to John Meltzer for initiating the translation work and for keeping it alive with his unstinting encouragement; to Clement Salaman for watching over the whole process with a kindly avuncular eye and for writing such a rich Preface; to Michael Shepherd for the spontaneity and vitality with which he put fingers to keyboard to produce such an inspiring piece of writing about the historical context of the work; to Adrian Bertoluzzi and Christophe Poncet for their generosity in supplying essential texts; to Nathan David for his open-hearted willingness to allow his beautiful sculptures to bring life to the book-jacket; to Jean Desebrock for her intelligent and sensitive handling of the format of the book; to Andrew Candy for designing such an attractive book-jacket; and to Anthony Werner, the publisher, for the exercise of his wonderful midwifery skills in bringing this book safely to the light of day.

Arthur Farndell

SOCRATES
(469-399 BC)

SOCRATES WROTE no books, founded no school, and accepted no disciples; but the impact he made upon the Athens of his time and upon subsequent generations of men and women all over the world is incalculable. His claim to know only that he knew nothing sits side by side with the declaration from the oracle at Delphi that there was no one wiser than Socrates.

Describing himself as 'a sort of gadfly given to the state by God', Socrates compares the state to 'a great and noble steed who is tardy in his motions ... and requires to be stirred into life'. He then speaks of his function in life: 'I am that gadfly which God has attached to the state, and all day long and in all places am always fastening upon you, arousing and persuading and reproaching you.'

Many readers of the dialogues in which Plato records the words of Socrates would agree that the 'gadfly' makes them feel uncomfortable and stirs them into life, for Socrates relentlessly and mercilessly challenges our basic preconceptions concerning ourselves and the way we live and move and have our being.

The unassuming Socrates, son of Sophroniscus the sculptor and Phaeranete the midwife, is the man who split the course of Greek philosophy in two: the pre-Socratic and all that came later. His insistence that we look at ourselves, at the workings of our minds, and at the way we conduct ourselves is a continuing impulse in Western civilisation.

PLATO
(*c.*428-*c.*348 BC)

ONE OF THE greatest philosophers ever to appear in the West, Plato exerted a notable influence upon his contemporaries through his intellectual and spiritual stature and through the Academy which he established in Athens. Here some of the foundations of European civilisation were prepared, as men and women, together with boys and girls, gathered to study geometry, arithmetic, music, and astronomy, and to contemplate the mysteries of being and becoming.

In all the centuries since, Plato's impact upon Western thought has been intensified and magnified through the spread of the dialogues which he composed. There are some thirty dialogues attributed to his hand. This volume contains commentaries to twenty-five of these dialogues, as well as commentaries to twelve letters thought to have been written by Plato.

These pages contain a consideration of the profound subjects over which Plato's mind ranged. These include Wisdom, the Good, Virtue, the Nature of Man, Prayer, Law, Holiness, Beauty, Friendship, Knowledge, Poetic Inspiration, Government, Temperance, and Courage.

WELCOME

THE GARDENS of Philosophy are ever open to all who would like to enter. Philosophy herself extends a hand in gracious welcome, inviting us to walk in the company of Plato and find peace and inspiration in an atmosphere of reflective inquiry.

Loving hands have tended these grounds throughout millennia. Our present guide is Marsilio Ficino, sometimes known as a second Plato. More than five hundred years ago his work in the philosophical gardens re-invigorated Europe through Latin translations of Plato's dialogues. The translations themselves were freshened by the streams of commentaries flowing from Ficino's heart and mind.

During the last hundred years new blooms have appeared in the gardens, as Ficino's own writings and translations have been rendered into modern European languages. The present floral offering consists of Ficino's shorter commentaries to Plato's dialogues, together with his commentaries to the twelve letters attributed to Plato.

There is no doubt that Ficino regarded Plato as one of the head gardeners, and himself as one who was privileged to work the same soil. Nevertheless, the ground tilled anew by Ficino has produced flowers attractive in their own right. Here is a welcoming posy, plucked here and there from the abundant beds:

'Man is a rational soul, partaking of mind and using a body.'

'Law is eternal, absolutely unchangeable, and among all nations it is the same.' *Not the Kwakjutls*

'The philosopher's function is to know the divine and govern the human.'

'Bodily beauty is not to be loved for its own sake but is to be thought of as an image of divine beauty.'

'Prayer is the ardent disposition of the pure soul, a disposition devoted to God and desirous of what is seen to be good.'

'The function of man is not to perceive, but to consider what he has perceived.'

May your visit be restful and restorative.

PART ONE

Summaries of Twenty-five
Dialogues of Plato

Translator's Notes to Part One

ADD

1. The word which Ficino uses to name a summary is 'epitome'. *and*

2. Part One contains twenty-five of these summaries or short commentaries. *equates them*

3. Ficino's longer works on individual dialogues are not included in this volume. *distinguishes them*

4. Ficino uses 'commentarium' to refer to an extended commentary, such as his work on *Parmenides*. *translations of*

5. For the reader who wishes to consult English works on the longer commentaries to Plato's dialogues, the following are available:

   Commentary on Plato's Symposium on Love, translated by Sears Jayne, Spring Publications, 1999.

   The Philebus Commentary, M.J.B. Allen, University of California Press, 1975; reprinted Medieval and Renaissance Texts and Studies, 2000.

   Marsilio Ficino and the Phaedran Charioteer, M.J.B. Allen, University of California Press, 1981.

   Icastes: Marsilio Ficino's Interpretation of Plato's 'Sophist', M.J.B. Allen, University of California Press, 1989.

6. Ficino's commentaries to the following dialogues are not yet available in English: *Parmenides, Timaeus, Republic, Laws,* and *Epinomis*.

7. It is not the aim of the translator to enter into the centuries-old debate concerning the authenticity of the works traditionally attributed to Plato. Almost every dialogue has been challenged at some time or another. The approach here is to present them all (including the somewhat mysterious *Philosophy*, alternatively called *The Lover*) with the spirit of simple acceptance which characterised Ficino's own approach. *of*

8. Part One begins with a Preface in which Ficino dedicates to Lorenzo de' Medici all of his work on Plato. The relief by Nathan David on which the jacket illustration is based was inspired by words from this Preface (see page 6).

date of pubn of combries / 1492

[Handwritten top margin:] Transl 2 diff Latin words as "household"
lares + domesticos — Joe D says its ok, skip it.
penes domesticos conquiescit p 1128
1129 line 2 Intra suos lares plurimum
educatum. Write this up at home!

[Handwritten left margin:] of top

The Preface to the Commentaries on Plato
by Marsilio Ficino of Florence,
Addressed to the Magnanimous
Lorenzo de' Medici

[Handwritten left:] also arguments

[Handwritten right:] = Op II. 1
p. 1129 ff.

Magnanimous Lorenzo:

DIVINE PROVIDENCE, which touches all things with its power
and arranges them harmoniously, has resolved not only to arm
holy religion with the Prophets, the Sibyls and the venerable Fathers,
but also to bestow on her alone the grace of a virtuous and excellent
philosophy, so that virtue herself, the source of everything good, would
at last go forth fearlessly among all who profess wisdom and eloquence, just as she dwells safely and peacefully in the heart of the
household. *[Handwritten: penes]* *[Handwritten: You get virtue from your household?]*
For it was proper that religion, the only path to happiness, should be *[Handwritten: not only]*
accessible to the sophisticated, just as she is to the simple. Under her *[Handwritten: but]*
guidance it is easier and safer for us to reach that bliss by whose grace *[Handwritten: generally]*
we have been born, that bliss which we are all striving to attain.

[Handwritten left margin: repetition] *[Handwritten: vulgaribus]*

And so, at the appointed time, almighty God sent down the divine
spirit of Plato from on high to shed the light of holy religion among all
nations through his wonderful life, innate powers, and eloquence. But
since the Platonic sun even up to our own time had not yet risen fully
upon the Latin-speaking peoples, Cosimo, the glory of Italy and a man
of outstanding devotion, striving to spread the Platonic light – a light
which is very propitious for religion – from the Greeks to those who
speak Latin, chose me, who had received much instruction within his
own household, for this great work. Now although I have been a
follower of the Platonic teaching from an early age, I entered upon this
serious task, not under my own auspices, but under those of your
grandfather Cosimo, trusting that divine aid would not be lacking for
so vital and godly an undertaking.

So, encouraged above all by this trust, I entered the Academy, and

[Handwritten left margin:] lares · says · intra lares totaleny · a different concept

3

[Handwritten bottom:] meaning started to read
Plato. Doesn't refer to
any institution, much less a building.

before Cosimo's death it was from there that I rendered ten of our Plato's dialogues into Latin for him. After Cosimo's death I gave your father, Piero – a most outstanding man – nine more dialogues to read. But after Piero had departed this life, fortune, often envious of noble works, dragged me away, against my will, from the work of translation. But you, a devotee of religion and a patron of philosophy, called me back, with every favour and assistance, to the task I had started. With fortune thus once more on my side, I returned to the undertaking; and I not only translated Plato's thought but sometimes I also summarised its content, and at other times, as far as I could, I explained it with brief commentaries.

And so this entire work, now completed through the help of God, I gladly dedicate to you.

These things, too, which were written for your forebears, belong by right of inheritance to you, the direct heir of your grandfather's excellence in cultivating our native land.

Now among the dialogues of Plato you will also read Plato's funeral oration, which was dedicated to your noble brother, Giuliano. Besides, when you come to the *Statesman* you will see that Federico, Duke of Urbino, was honoured by me on the day he himself paid homage to your palace.

However, not only do the thirty-seven books inscribed with your name belong to you, but so do all the others as well, since they were all completed by your grace; and I, too, am yours.

But I do not claim to have fully expressed Plato's language in these books, nor do I believe that it can ever be fully expressed by anyone, however learned. I say that his language resembles a divine pronouncement rather than human speech: often thundering on high, often flowing with the sweetness of nectar, but always encompassing the heavenly mysteries.

Indeed, just as the world is endowed with three gifts in particular – usefulness, order, and embellishment – and through these gives witness to us of the divine craftsman, so Plato's language, containing the creation, rejoices in three special gifts: the philosophical usefulness of its judgements, the rhetorical order of its structure and flow, and the embellishment of its floral poetry. At all points Plato's language calls upon divine witnesses and provides irrefutable proof of God, the architect of creation.

Therefore, magnanimous Lorenzo, may all prosper greatly who earnestly seek from Plato the most detailed regulations for the upbringing of the young. Let others instruct the less mature, and let the enlightened eventually approach the Platonic gateway, so that they may finally bring back from there divine mysteries rather than childish instruction. I have just said 'finally', Lorenzo, for prior to setting forth the divine pronouncements, our Plato, to prevent what is sacred from becoming available to the profane, leads the minds of his heroes step by step to the summit of the threefold pathway of purification, detach-ment, and return to source.

Thus Plato's words have much on purifying souls of disturbances; more on detaching minds from the senses; and most of all on turning minds both to themselves and to God, the Author of all. Once duly turned to Him, as if to the sun, they are blissfully enlightened by the rays of truth which they have been seeking.

However, while our Plato often describes the true function of man in a veiled manner, he is seen at times to jest and play games; but Plato's games and jests carry far more weight than the serious discourses of the Stoics. For he does not scorn to touch upon what is lowly in any place, provided that, by captivating his more lowly hearers in a gentle way, he may lead them the more easily to the heights.

With weighty intent he often mixes the useful with the sweet, so that by the gentle charm of persuasive words he may through the very bait of pleasure entice to wholesome food those minds which by nature are rather inclined to pleasure.

Plato often tells fables in the manner of a prophet, since his style seems to be not so much that of a philosopher as that of a prophet. For from time to time he rages and rambles like a prophet, following no human pattern but one that is prophetic and divine. He plays the part not so much of a teacher as of a priest and a prophet, sometimes raving but sometimes purifying others and carrying them off into the same divine frenzy. But in all this he clearly uses fables for one particular purpose: that while all may find delight among the varied flowers of the Academy, only the purified may gather the fruits and enjoy their sweet taste, their easy assimilation, and the perfect nourish-ment they provide.

Now Plato presents everything in dialogues so that the living word may bring the speakers before our eyes, to persuade us more power-fully and move us more deeply. Moreover, in his dialogues Plato takes the opportunity to honour his friends as is fitting, naturally com-mending many of them to posterity. Again, in a dialogue it is easier to

Strong use of Academy for the field of Philosophy

dialog

examine different views on a particular subject. I should add that a dialogue gives delight through its wonderful richness, and through its attractive power it holds both hearer and reader.

But why spend longer on trivial details?

myth of minerva

Magnanimous Lorenzo, Wisdom born from Jove's head alone was with him from the beginning, fashioning all things. Like her father, she too gave birth to a daughter from her head alone, a daughter named Philosophy, who would delight in being with the sons of men.

Wisdom 9

So this is why, in former times, men of true worth everywhere strove to attain her as she travelled through the different nations upon earth. Of all these men our Plato not only strove after her but was the first and only one to worship her fully. For in acknowledging her holiness, he was the first to wreathe her brow with the priestly garland and to robe her in a gown worthy of the noble daughter of Minerva. Then he anointed her head, hands, and feet with fragrant perfumes. Finally, wherever the spirit of Philosophy trod, he strewed her path with a colourful carpet of flowers.

Such was, and still is, the appearance and apparel of this goddess walking within the precincts of the Academy. But whenever she strays outside the gardens of the Academy, not only does she always lose her perfumes and flowers, but – horrible to relate! – she often falls among thieves, and losing the trappings of priesthood and dignity, she wanders hither and thither, naked and as if unholy; and she appears so marred that she is no longer pleasing to her companions, Phoebus and Mercury, or approved of by her grandfather, Jove, or by her mother, Minerva. Yet when she follows her mother's counsel and takes refuge within the walls and gardens of the Academy, she recovers her former dignity, and there, as though at home, she happily comes to rest.

This is why, Platonic Lorenzo, she delights in encouraging all, including yourself, who want to learn and to live well to enter the Platonic Academy. For this is where young people will cheerfully and easily follow good principles of living while they jest, and practise the art of discussion while they play. This is where men, too, will become thoroughly conversant with the knowledge of matters both private and public. This is where old men will hope to exchange their mortal life for life eternal.

In the gardens of the Academy poets will hear Apollo singing beneath the laurels.

In the forecourt of the Academy orators will behold Mercury declaiming.

academy sounds like an institution

// illustr on dust jacket

Presumably F. means that Plato touches upon all these subjects.

PREFACE TO THE COMMENTARIES ON PLATO

In the porch and hall lawyers and statesmen will listen to Jove himself as he ordains laws, pronounces justice, and governs empires.

Finally, within the innermost sanctuary philosophers will recognise their Saturn as he contemplates the secrets of the heavens. *? See 21, 22*

But everywhere priests and guardians of what is sacred will find the weapons with which to defend religion vigorously against the attacks of the wicked. *astronomical*

So come here, I beseech you, all you who pursue the ways of liberation; come here, for here you will reach your journey's end and attain the freedom of life; and all of you who are afire with the unquenchable desire to follow truth and to seek happiness, gather here without delay, for here, with God's blessing, you will come to know truth and bliss in accordance with your promise. *heavens? that World-soul Urania was the god*

But take care not to disseminate your views on matters Platonic, or rather divine, without due consideration, but make your judgement after a thorough and balanced examination; and do not direct any malicious criticism towards those who, without the slightest trace of malice, watch over you and work for you. But rather be happy to look favourably upon the wise author and also upon the translator, who has taken the utmost care to work for the common good of all, not only by translating the words but also by expounding the meanings. *of astro heavens as well) as being the World Soul, no, the*

I beg you not to be so harsh as to censure and suppress the ancient teaching of liberation which, alas, has already been suppressed for far too long, but which by divine providence has recently emerged into the light; no misguided mortal should wish to bring to nought what almighty God wills to live everywhere. For the right hand of the Lord has created Virtue; the right hand of the Lord has now exalted her. She shall not die, but she shall live and declare the works of the Lord. *Divine mind. ?*

But, excellent Lorenzo, to what end has our great love for Plato – a love which knows no bounds – taken hold of us? Have we spoken eloquently on behalf of Plato, the Prince of eloquence? No; for he has spoken sufficiently, even abundantly, on his own behalf, especially to those who, free from agitation, prove themselves to be impartial hearers. *knowledge & peace ego & with God exalting virtue)*

But I have no need to encourage you now, for in all these matters you are amazingly supportive by inclination, responsive by nature, and instructed by study. And so I shall simply wish you happy reading and a very happy life.

Remember your Marsilio.

But when I name Marsilio Ficino, understand that Filippo Valori of

Shd explain who Valori is
I believe he financed this among
other subjects

our Academy is also named at the same time. For if Valori and Marsilio are united in defending Plato and in loving you, they are certainly united to each other.

Valori's outstanding goodness commends him to you, Lorenzo; his reputation as a Platonist exalts him; his extraordinary love for you commits him fully to your care.

in service of
moral optimism

50

Summary of Plato's *Hipparchus*

PLATO'S INTENTION in *Hipparchus* is to teach us that all men strive after the Good, since even those who seem to go astray through greed are also striving after the Good. Because they desire gain, gain is useful; but the useful is good, and therefore they desire the Good. For gain is the opposite of loss; but since gain is opposed to evil it is the opposite of evil. The opposite of evil is the Good: therefore gain is the Good. For this reason, since even those who seem to fall away from striving for the Good desire the Good, nothing now militates against the fact that all men strive after the Good.

Now the Good is twofold: the first aspect is the end, the second the means to the end. The first is to be sought for its own sake, the second for the sake of something else. The desire for the first is will; the desire for the second is choice. The first is to be honoured, while the second is useful. We enjoy the first, but we use the second. Acquisition of the first is called happiness, and acquisition of the second is called gain. Gain is therefore the useful acquisition of the good, which is conducive to honouring the Good. But if it does not lead to this it is not useful, nor is its acquisition a gain. Thus the desire for gain is praiseworthy, a desire which nature has implanted within all. However, that false view should be rejected which, ignoring what is truly useful and profitable, twists the natural desire towards its opposite.

All these things Plato teaches secretly, while Socrates refutes, by induction and reasoning, the false opinions which Hipparchus puts forward concerning the desire for gain. However, Plato treats as self-evident the proposition that all men strive after the Good, to conclude that all by nature strive after gain and that this natural striving is praiseworthy. Now this is the conclusion which Socrates puts forward in an indirect way through three methods of argument: example, induction, and reasoning. But conversely, from this whole argument from the particular, we gather that that proposition is fully confirmed. Clearly, all men strive after the Good, and that is the final aim of this book, for the first aim is to show that all are desirous of gain and that gain is not to be despised.

Summary of Plato's Book on
Philosophy or *The Lover*

Intro says dubious

THE HEART OF this dialogue is the definition of the Philosopher's function. Now the Philosopher's function is to know the divine and govern the human: the first aspect includes contemplative Philosophy, while the second embraces practical Philosophy.

Thus the Philosopher first contemplates, through wisdom, the divine or absolute nature of the Good. Then he governs human affairs by directing men's activities towards their end in this Good. But there are two prerequisites for this. The first is a recognition of what human nature is and how it is delivered from evil and led to the Good: this condition the Philosopher meets through insight. The second is putting in order people's attitudes and actions, moderating and restraining them in such a way that they easily incline towards the Good, which wisdom has discovered and to which insight has shown them the way. This is accomplished through the moral virtues, which are all subsumed by Plato in the one name of Justice. The government of human affairs rests on these two conditions.

Now it is the work of the Philosopher to understand that a single man governs both family and state. Thus one practising the moral virtues would be the ideal householder, and the same person, practising the civil virtues, would be the ideal king. *King needn't*

The conclusion is thus reached that the function of the Philosopher comprises all these: wisdom, insight, justice, and the virtues moral, domestic, civic, and kingly. Through wisdom he comes to know the divine; through insight and justice he governs human affairs, as he orders his own life, that of his family, and that of the state. Such is the work of the Philosopher, which Plato expounds more fully in the books of the *Republic* and which he indicates but briefly in this book.

Before that, however, he refutes two views held by others about the function of the Philosopher. The first was held by Solon, who asserted that the function was to learn as much as possible. The second was held by Hippias the Sophist, who maintained that it was expertise in all the arts. Once these have been refuted, Plato briefly alludes to the view that we have just mentioned.

Thus Socrates, in opposition to two of Dionysius' followers, is portrayed as having debated this topic in the schools of Dionysius, who taught Plato the elements of grammar, and then, within the circle of his own friends, as reviewing from the beginning those subjects which he had investigated in the schools.

have moral virtues, just civic!

Summary of *Theages*, Concerning Wisdom

I N THIS DIALOGUE Wisdom is defined, and the last part of the definition is chosen for examination, so that it may be clear how it is acquired by human beings. In the first part Wisdom is said to be twofold: absolute and conditioned. Absolute Wisdom is that which is named Wisdom simply and without any addition. Conditioned Wisdom is that which is said to be not simply Wisdom but some sort of Wisdom.

This is how the first is defined: awareness of those things of which it is possible to have knowledge. Now knowledge is of those things which are ever the same and of the same quality, such as the highest principles of creation and the eternal causes of all things; but these things are called divine, and thus Wisdom is the knowledge of divine matters, and this indeed is absolute Wisdom.

Conditioned Wisdom, however, is common to all arts and skills, for the highest point of any art is called a kind of Wisdom, such as the Wisdom of the helmsman, the Wisdom of the charioteer, and the Wisdom of the soldier. Now of all those arts which are given the additional name of Wisdom, there is a special one which employs the others as servants, and this is the Wisdom of citizenship.

Indeed, this skill is defined as the one which unites the common good of the state and the common good of nations. It is called both a civil discipline and a royal discipline. Its subject is the state; its end is the common good; its servants are all the arts. It has two duties: to establish laws, and to carry them out once they have been established. The first duty acts through the providence of the law-giver, the second through the lawful justice of the courts.

Now in very many of his dialogues Plato reflects upon the question of how someone obtains civil wisdom; and in the present dialogue, called *Theages*, he considers whether it is taught by citizens, or by Sophists, or by purely contemplative philosophers. In *Meno*, as well as here, he denies to some extent that it is learnt from citizens, or even

12

from Sophists, or from those devoted to contemplation alone, because the first group have never taught even their own children; the second group do not have any regard for the Good; and the third group have no experience of human affairs. The remaining possibilities, therefore, are that it is perceived by those philosophers who are especially experienced both in contemplation and in action, or that it happens by divine fate. Such philosophers are nowhere to be found. For this reason, in *Meno* as well as in *Theages*, he asserts that it happens by divine gift that the providence of God imparts to the restrained minds of citizens the understanding of the Good itself as well as the laws which lead to that Good. Indeed, he calls this idea civil wisdom in *Theages*, while in *Meno*, in place of the earlier term, he calls it a kind of prophecy, and he compares citizens to people in a frenzy. He often says, too, that the human race will never desist from evils unless true philosophers rule or unless those who govern the state become philosophers by some divine intervention.

Now in this book, when Socrates had defined the two parts of Wisdom and had said, with a kind of irony, that Theages could not obtain this civil wisdom either from citizens, or from Sophists, or from himself as a philosopher devoted to contemplation, he added that the power of the daemon should be put to the test and that the will of God should then be implored with prayers, as if such prayers might be learnt in this way and the providence of God might frequently impart to men, through the intermediate spirits, the divine pronouncements of what needs to be done.

Now Dionysius the Areopagite gives the name 'Principalities' to those servants who, at the command of God, inspire the minds of good citizens and true princes to govern well. This would perhaps afford an opportunity to discuss the daemon of Socrates, but the brevity of a summary prevents this. In fact, Maximus Tyrius and Hermes and Apuleius have discoursed at length on this. But Plato presents three people here: the Athenian citizen Demodocus, together with his son Theages, who is striving for Wisdom, and Socrates. The dialogue begins with a request from Demodocus.

13

Summary of *Meno*,
Concerning Virtue

T HERE ARE FOUR kinds of method used by Plato: example,
assumption, reasoning, and reflection; and how these come about
is clearly shown in the abridgement of *Alcinous*, which we have
also translated. There we find three types of Platonic dialogue; and
his practice is to use specific methods for specific dialogues. For one
dialogue will merely ask questions and refute falsehood; another will
merely expound and teach the truth; another will be focused on the
One. The first is enquiring and contentious; the second is expository;
the last is called a combination.

Now although *Meno* is a combination, for the most part it investigates and refutes, and it touches upon all these methods. In order that
no one who is gathering the meanings from the other dialogues of
Plato which pertain to exposition rather than to inquiry and who turns
his attention to this *Meno* should find it difficult to elicit the main point
of this debate, it is this: to investigate what virtue is and how it is
present amongst us. This Socrates does while he refutes the four definitions of virtue given by Meno, Aristippus, Gorgias, and Prodicus; and,
with two objections, he retracts his own definition, which was given
after those four. Indeed, the truth shines forth from the refutation of
falsehood.

Now the virtue of man is the disposition of the soul by which his
natural power performs its work in the best possible way: this definition is given in the books of the *Republic*. The work of any power is
performed best when it is directed towards its own end. What leads to
this end is said to be useful. It is right, therefore, that in this dialogue
the general office of virtue is said to be that it surrenders actions as well
as the useful things which we employ when acting. That definition,
therefore, is in harmony with this dialogue and is common to all the
virtues. On account of the diversity of the powers of the soul and of
actions there are indeed very many kinds of virtues, among which the

one which is described as the common principle of virtue always receives consideration.

The first power of the soul is the mind, whose action is the eternal contemplation of truth. The second power is reason, whose action is the investigation of truth. The third power is imagination, whose action is to gather those things which the senses, its messengers, present, and through those things to hold discourse. Now these are the three powers of the soul which are called cognitive.

There remain three others, which are called appetitive: will, the power of anger, and the power of passion. The action of will is to desire what mind and reason present. The action of anger is to approach what reason and imagination propose. The action of passion is to accept what imagination and the senses place before it.

Furthermore, there are two powers subordinate to these six: the power to move and the power to take nourishment; but, as far as virtue is concerned, these two share nothing, or only a very little, with the higher powers.

The disposition of mind which perfects contemplation is wisdom. What perfects the investigation of reason is knowledge and prudence. Knowledge, indeed, perfects the investigation of those things which nature creates, while prudence perfects the consideration of those things which we do. The disposition which perfects the discourse of the imagination is right opinion, which is, in fact, called sagacity. Justice and liberality perfect the will. Courage and its handmaidens perfect anger. Continence, together with temperance, perfects passion. What is common to all these is a disposition which perfects the action of the natural power and makes it fitting and useful for attaining its ultimate end.

Now the different virtues are also considered in different ways. For wisdom is by nature the eternal union of all principles within the mind and the everlasting contemplation of truth. Knowledge is gained through the teaching of philosophy, which gives proof of remembrance, while reason, which once cast off its wings, recovers them by turning towards the mind through remembering. Prudence comes through teaching and long practice. Right opinion comes through examples, authority, induction, and destiny. Justice and courage and temperance, and the other moral virtues of prudence and right opinion, are perfected by laws and lawful practice.

Hence Plato put forward these two – prudence and right opinion – as the beginnings of the moral virtues. For this reason, prudence, in the

15

Prudence

writings of Plato, often takes on the name of all moral virtues; and there is a virtue pertaining to right opinion which is called civil expertise, by which rightful princes and citizens, honourable in their actions, take care of the public good, even though they are not experienced in contemplation. In *Theages*, as well as in the present *Meno*, Plato maintains that this ability is not given to citizens except by divine ordinance.

And so, anyone who would understand Plato's intention in *Meno* from this small summary will reject contradictions and avoid objections by first setting out a definition of this kind. It is not right, when giving the subject matter, to deal with that dispute about remembrance and geometric figures, for it was inserted as an accessory and not as the main theme. A summary, however, needs only the central point. Indeed, it is the duty of a commentary, rather than of a summary, to discuss details.

parallel Dante's aute purgatory

dismisses a problem

Presumably this would be his example of a slave quickly learning the properties of geometric figures as proof that slave already knew them & needed only to remember them.

16

Summary of *Alcibiades I*,
Concerning the Nature of Man

OUR PLATO'S illuminating book, which is entitled *Alcibiades I*, more charming than Alcibiades himself and more precious than all gold, teaches what man is and what his duty is.

"Now man is a rational soul, partaking of mind and using a body." From this definition is derived his threefold duty: for as he is a rational soul, he is turned back to himself by giving attention to himself through the circle of reasoning; as he partakes of mind, he flows back into the divine mind as a stream to its source; as he uses a body, he applies himself to governing human affairs.

Therefore the full, absolute duty of man is firstly to attend to his own nature, and secondly to turn from that, as from an image and effect, to the divine mind, his origin and cause. When his mind is illuminated by the divine mind, man perceives the absolute nature of the good, the useful, the beautiful, and the just; and he fully understands what is good, useful, beautiful, and just within himself. Hence he knows what is good and what is useful in others with whom he deals or whom he rules. And when he knows the absolute Good, his own good, and the good of others, he must take steps towards caring for himself and for every other person, according to the measure of the good that is recognised.

what good would that do?

It is necessary for him to study moral and mathematical philosophy, and theology, in order to return to himself and to the mind, which is his cause. Moral and mathematical training restores the soul, which has been immersed in the body, to itself; theology seizes it and raises it beyond itself into God.

ans.

That's not what you said in Meno.

Consciousness of the divine mind and of ideal forms is called wisdom. Knowledge of oneself, and the discovery of the good and the useful in oneself and in one's fellows, emanating from the observation of the divine mind, is called prudence. As it perceives the good, prudence clearly directs human actions, both public and private, towards the best end. As it perceives the useful, it directs actions through the

Ficino's distinctive twist

[it?]? is?,

2nd use

this dichotomy

It is !?!

17

ch-transl. Could it be from the GIFT of the divine mind? For how can a mere man observe divine m..?

Vague & unclear

?

appropriate means and the right ways to attain this end. As it perceives the beautiful, it ordains the sequence and the way to be followed in this development as if on a journey. As it perceives the just, it prescribes the parameters of individual works, the regulations of the imposed sequence, the punishment for transgressing the law of this journey, and the reward for keeping this law.

There is, therefore, a movement from philosophy to wisdom, and from wisdom to prudence. Now prudence, the mistress of life, bestows her own discipline, the discipline of everything in the household, and the discipline of the state. Man governs through prudence, while the home and the state are preserved through public friendship and justice. I call public friendship that agreement by which all willingly assemble under the same law and the same leader and look towards the same end. I call public justice that lawful discrimination by which individuals progress, albeit by different paths, under the same leader and towards the same end, which is the public good; keep the varied allocation of duties assigned by nature and the laws, according to the nature and nobility of each one; and fulfil their own function without usurping that of another.

differentiation

Within this dialogue there are two theological expressions: 'the Self as the Self' and 'the Self as individual'. For man, the first expression indicates the soul within Idea, and the second refers to the soul within the body.

But more of this in the commentaries, which I have already begun to write, on these ten dialogues of Plato.

Summary of *Alcibiades II*,
Concerning Prayer

S INCE *ALCIBIADES II*, a most holy book, is entitled 'concerning Prayer', one may briefly gather the nature of prayer, as well as what is to be asked for in prayer, when, and how.

The following definition of prayer is taken partly from Orpheus and partly from Plato: prayer is the ardent disposition of the pure soul, a disposition devoted to God and desirous of what is seen to be good. To this disposition Zoroaster and Orpheus added fumes from under the earth and symbols whenever prayers were directed to the secondary deities. When Hermes and Plato worshipped the majesty of the supreme godhead, they removed all external rituals, leaving only the pure fragrance of the soul. But we have written more fully on all these matters in our commentaries. *suffumigations but sounds like the gas that Inspired the Delphic Oracle.*

As to what should be asked for in prayer, Plato declares it to be the Good, and this is clear from the fact that, on the evidence of the Poet and of the Spartans, he approves of this prayer and he thinks that it is safe for the prudent man and for the imprudent man, and that a prayer of this kind can be made by anyone at any time. But a request for any particular individual good is safe only when the person has followed prudence; otherwise it is dangerous. Here he speaks many words about prudence, which I beseech you, Cosimo, the most prudent of all men, to read carefully, that you may understand directly how much he values prudence.

Universal prayer, therefore, by which the Good alone is sought, can be made at any time; but an individual prayer, by which something particular which is seen to be good is desired, should be made when the person knows what is to be asked for. He will know this when he understands what is good and what is evil. This he will understand when he has learnt it from mind. He will learn it when he turns towards mind. He will turn when he has purified his soul and driven away the darkness. He will purify his soul when he has surrendered himself to lawful philosophy. He will make this surrender when he *that word*

again! more approp-riate here than previ-ously.

19

recognises his ignorance. Therefore the inscription on the temple of Apollo was 'Know thyself', lest anyone should rashly approach God in prayer.

Now in an individual prayer, what should be prayed for and in what sequence was taught by Hermes in his *Prayers*, by Orpheus in his *Hymns*, and by Pythagoras in his *Golden Verses*; their ceremonies we shall expound elsewhere.

Then Plato, imitating these theologians, in his book on beauty introduces Socrates praying thus: 'Kindly Pan, and you other gods, grant, I beseech you, that I may be made beautiful within and that everything outside me may become dear within me. May I consider only the wise man to be rich. Bestow as much of this gold as none but a temperate man may bear or take away.'

What does Socrates seek? The good. Which good? Wisdom, that is, consciousness of divine truth, which God alone can grant, which the beautiful soul alone is strong enough to receive, the soul that is temperate, pure, and bright. What does he ask for first? That wisdom may make him worthy. It is certainly the action of a rash man to ask for any gift of which he is unworthy.

Who is worthy of divine wisdom? Who is ready to bear its light, who is ready? The man who firstly through continence, secondly through temperance, and finally through holiness, that is, through the civil and purifying virtue of the purified soul, has cleansed his soul, so that he has become beautiful, that is, totally pure and clear, and has chosen virtue, divine wisdom alone, the treasury of all riches, as his model.

For this reason Socrates beseeches God, the Father of all, and His servants to breathe favourably upon him, that he may be cleansed by their kind and gracious favour. But he passes lightly over bodily and external matters, choosing to have those things which do not hinder the tranquil purity of the soul. Then, when this beauty has been imparted, he prays that he may consider wisdom alone, the awareness of God, to be all wealth and sufficiency, and that he may thirst for that alone.

Finally, as if prepared through the words already spoken, he asks for this shining gold of divine wisdom. He does not ask proudly, nor yet mildly. Indeed, intemperate men are granted very little consciousness of truth; but God embraces within Himself the whole of this limitless consciousness, and a temperate man obtains a large and full measure. Therefore he has asked for as much of this gold as only a temperate man is able to carry. Indeed, I believe that this is the burning gold which John, in *Revelation*, advises us to buy.

20

Summary of *Minos*,
Concerning Law

*M*INOS ENQUIRES into law, so that we may understand, in a few words, how many kinds there are and where law comes from. Anyone who carefully attends to Plato's words in this book on law and in the books called the *Laws*, as well as in the *Republic*, will describe law with the following universal definition: Law is the true principle of governing, which directs what is governed to the best end through appropriate means, apportioning punishment to the transgressor and reward to the obedient. Hence it comes about that when the institutions of princes are not true and do not lead straight to the best, they are not laws: they are decrees, edicts, and institutes rather than laws. For, indeed, from a law a lawful work often becomes famous; from a lawful work, a just one; from a just work, a work that is good, right, and true.

For this reason it is necessary for law to be true and good. It also follows that law is eternal, absolutely unchangeable, and among all nations it is the same on the same matters, provided it is true in this way; for that which changes according to time, place, and opinion is not called law but an institute.

Now there are four kinds of law, as can be gathered from *Timaeus*, *Phaedrus*, and *Gorgias*. The first kind, which Plato calls providence, is divine. The second, which he calls fate, is celestial. The third, which he calls nature, is the moving. The fourth, which he calls natural prudence, is human. *Th transl the movers le*

The first kind of law, which Orpheus and Plato consider the law of Saturn, is in the divine mind. The second, which they consider the law of Jupiter, is in the higher part of the World Soul. The third, which they hold to be the law of the first Venus, is in the moving and lower power of the World Soul. Finally, they call law in the mind of man the law of the second Venus. *why these planets alone?*

The first flows forth from the supreme Good, which is above mind; the second, from mind and the supreme Good; the third, from the

This might explain that reference to Saturn as being ruler of all and the supreme good or whatever it was, p.7

21

stupid! no diff between 3 + 4!

supreme Good, mind, and universal soul; the fourth, likewise, from the supreme Good, mind, and soul.

All these kinds, however, turn back again to the Good itself: the first, in ideas, around the supreme Good, above principles; the second, in principles, around ideas, above elements; the third, in elements, around principles, above forms; the fourth, in concepts, around principles, above acts and arts, and this they call the royal law, because it represents the King eternal.

The origin of law is ascertained from what has been said. Indeed, as has been stated, all the kinds of law emanate, albeit in different ways, from the Creator of the universe. For this reason all the illustrious lawgivers have ascribed the discovery of laws to God, but through different names and means. Zoroaster, lawgiver to the Bactrians and Persians, acknowledged Horomasis; Trismegistus, lawgiver to the Egyptians, acknowledged Hermes; Moses, lawgiver to the Hebrews, most justly referred to God, the Father of all creation; Minos, lawgiver to the Cretans, referred to Jupiter; Charondas, lawgiver to the Carthaginians, acknowledged Saturn; Lycurgus, lawgiver to the Spartans, Apollo; Draco and Solon, lawgivers to the Athenians, Minerva; Pompilius, lawgiver to the Romans, Aegeria; Mahommed, lawgiver to the Arabs, Gabriel; Zamolxis, lawgiver to the Scythians, Vesta; our Plato, lawgiver to the Magnesians and the Siculians, acknowledged Jupiter and Apollo. However, when the Arcadians, the Thebans, and the Cyreniacs asked for laws, Plato refused their requests.

Summary of *Euthyphro*,
Concerning Holiness *nota classical virtue.*

*E*UTHYPHRO IS WHOLLY controversial. This is because some followers of Plato have called this book into dispute, just as they have *Euthydemus* and *Hippias*. But in truth, while Socrates refutes the false opinions of Euthyphro concerning holiness, he indicates, for those hunting the truth, the tracks that lead to holiness.

In this book, therefore, as well as in *Gorgias*, Plato gives the name 'holiness' to that part of justice which attributes to God what is His own when one renders to God what has been received directly from God. As Plato argues in his book *On Nature*, we have received our body from the four elements, the natural constitution of our species from the celestial spheres, the parts of the soul which are drawn by desires from the daemons and the souls of the constellations and spheres, but reason and mind, the image of our Father, we have received from the Creator of the whole world Himself without any ministry from the heavenly host or the daemons. Therefore these are of God, these are to be given back to God, and this repayment, which is preceded by piety and followed by religion, is called holiness. For piety is the acknowledgement of God the Father. Holiness is the repayment to the acknowledged God of what is God's. Religion is the indissoluble binding to God Himself of what has been given back to God, by faithful meditation and just works.

This is why that wise man rightly said that a triple-corded rope is difficult to undo, a rope plaited from piety, holiness, and religion. Piety arouses holiness. Holiness confirms and sanctions piety. Holiness also stirs religion. Religion binds holiness. For before this, by impulse, inspiration, or admonition, we need to consider with an undoubting faith, which they call piety, that the one God is our Father. Anyone who has understood these things soon applies the full force of his mind and reason to knowing and loving God. And this constant intention to know and love the Godhead Hermes also calls holiness. From this eager directing of the attention towards God, and from the ardour of the mind, it comes about that we meditate on, and engage in, all the works of God and His institutes and commandments, and with constant zeal we practise whatever pertains to His worship. And so, binding ourselves to God through this practice, we are religious.

Now with this definition and distinction before us, what Plato says about holiness in *Euthyphro* and elsewhere becomes clear. And when what is loved by God is said to be holy, this is true; but it is because it is holy that it is loved by God, not that it is holy because it is loved. And because it is loved it is beloved, since what is holy and what is beloved are not exactly the same. For the principles of holiness do not consist in being loved, but rather in surrender and devotion.

Moreover, when it is said that the function of holiness is to be the handmaiden of God, the words are true, but to which work of God is it the handmaiden? To the conversion of the soul. For the work of God is to create, to convert, to purify, to illuminate, to perfect. As soon as God, by His inspiration, begins to convert the soul to Himself through the impulse of piety, that assent by which the soul freely restores itself to God, who is converting it, is called holiness, which is indeed the handmaiden of God in perfecting the conversion.

Finally, it is added that holiness, the knowledge of praying and sacrificing to God, belongs particularly to religion, which, as we have said, accompanies holiness. By praying, the soul seeks; by sacrificing, it gives. What does it seek from God? Itself. What does it give to God? Itself. It seeks the ideal form which is in the divine mind, and which Hermes sought from Pimander; but it gives its own nature, which partakes of the ideal form.

Hippias or *On the Beautiful and Noble*: Summary Dedicated to Piero de' Medici, Father of His People

BEAUTY IS DISCUSSED in the *Phaedrus*, the *Symposium*, and *Hippias*. In *Hippias* Socrates opposes Hippias, the Sophist, who, though he knew not, believed that he knew.

This 'not knowing' renders the mind impervious to instruction; and so, instead of teaching what beauty is, Socrates shows what it is not and refutes false opinions. He defines a Sophist as a man who, for the sake of money and honour, strives to seem wise rather than to be wise. This is how Hippias is described in the prologue and at the end of the prologue.

Taking his cue from one of the speeches of Hippias on the subject of noble duties, Socrates asks what that intrinsic beauty is by which everything else becomes beautiful. For particulars must be referred to the universal inherent in them, and the universal which is inherent in particulars must be referred to that universal which transcends particulars.

For individual noble men are rendered noble by the beauty which is common to all of them, but the beauty common to the many is imprinted by divine nature, just as a symbol is imprinted by a seal. Each multiplicity is referred to the one which is inherent in it, and this inherent one is referred to the one which transcends multiplicity.

Since many things are beautiful, each must be beautiful on account of the beauty common to them all and inherent in them all; and the beauty which is within them all, being within something other and not within itself, must depend on something other and not on itself.

Each and every beautiful thing Plato calls 'this particular beauty'; the beauty within all things he calls 'beauty'; and the beauty and Idea that is above all he calls 'Beauty itself'. The first is appreciated by sense and opinion. The second is cognised by reason. The third is perceived by mind.

When asked, Hippias gives three definitions based on sense and opinion. After refuting these, Socrates also gives three definitions: two based on reason, and the third based on mind. For the Sophist proceeds on the basis of sense and opinion, while the philosopher proceeds on the basis of reason and mind.

Initially, Hippias replies that a beautiful maiden is Beauty itself. This is shown to be false by the fact that it is not by virtue of the maiden that all beautiful things have become beautiful. And the maiden is beautiful if compared to brutes, but unsightly if compared to divine beings. And so she seems to be equally beautiful and unsightly.

Then Hippias replies in like manner, saying that any particular beautiful thing is not common. Gold is Beauty itself, by which all things are made beautiful. Socrates refutes this, because some of the things that gold mixes with become beautiful and others become ugly. Therefore Beauty itself not only makes things beautiful but also ennobles them. This is why whatever adorns does so as much for the sake of what it is adorning as for its own sake. Gold is not the only substance to adorn things: others are silver and ivory and such like.

Thirdly, Hippias infers something specific rather than general. He says that being beautiful is: being healthy in body, being rich and receiving honours, dying in old age, and being buried by one's sons, having already buried one's own parents. This is clearly false because, apart from men, nothing else is made beautiful by this kind of beauty; and, besides, what may be beautiful for men may be unseemly for gods and their offspring, for in their case parents do not die.

Having refuted these arguments adduced by Hippias concerning individual physical things as appreciated by the senses and by opinion, Socrates now moves towards higher things and introduces the subject of that which reason presents to opinion, rather than that which sense presents to opinion. For first of all Hippias says that the beautiful is the seemly. Indeed, whatever is non-physical is greater and also common to a greater number of things.

But Socrates refutes this with the following analysis. Seemliness offers the choice of merely seeming beautiful or of both seeming and being. If you say the first, then seemliness appears as a deception about the beautiful rather than Beauty itself. For true beauty makes things beautiful, just as true greatness, even though it be not seen, makes things great. If you say the second, you speak falsely. For if Beauty itself were to grant a beautiful appearance every time it bestows being, then all beautiful things would appear to everyone just as they are. We are shown that this is false by the debates and disputes about beautiful things.

Then he adduces another view which reason presents to opinion. The useful is what he next identifies as the beautiful. Usefulness is non-physical and is common to many things. And it is not surprising that thinking about what is seemly and useful can be deceptive. For the seemly has an order that relates one part to another, and the parts to the whole, while the useful has an order that relates one whole to another; and order seems to represent beauty. Thus it is easy for anyone to take the seemly or the useful as the beautiful.

It has been established already that the seemly is not the beautiful. He now shows that the useful is not the beautiful. The useful has the power to do something. Thus power and usefulness are the same thing. Whatever we do, we do it through some power, but for the most part we do bad things; and so, by and large, power and usefulness import evil, but beauty is never a cause of evil. Therefore mere usefulness is not beauty.

'But at least it contributes to the good,' someone will answer; and the counter-argument is: Because the profitable tends towards the good, the profitable makes the good. Because that which makes is different from that which is made, the profitable is different from the good. The profitable and the beautiful are the same, and therefore the beautiful and the good are different. Thus the beautiful is not the good, and the good is not the beautiful, which is downright absurd.

Finally, when the errors of sense, of opinion, and of thought have been refuted, mind makes it clear to reason that beauty is a kind of grace, which moves and attracts the soul by means of mind, sight, and hearing. This, of course, is ascertained partly from the end of this dialogue and partly from Plato's *Phaedrus* and *Symposium*.

'By what cause is this grace present?' asks Socrates. 'And by what name is it to be called?' And he does not tell the conceited Sophist what he revealed to Phaedrus and to Agathon, who, though ignorant, acknowledged their ignorance and were amenable to his teaching.

Grace is indeed beauty, not on the basis of sense, for sense would not concur with mind but would be compatible with the other senses such as hearing and sight; not on the basis of mind, for mind would shun eyes and ears; not on the basis of pleasure, for pleasure is found not in hearing and seeing only, but in all the senses; not on the basis of hearing alone, for hearing would not concur with mind and sight; not on the basis of sight, for sight would not be present in hearing and mind; and not on the basis of hearing and seeing simultaneously, for then beauty would be present in the combination of sight and hearing. In any one of these, divorced from the activity of the others, there is no beauty.

We say, however, that that grace is perceived by three powers of the soul and is present jointly within the three objects of their perception. For this reason he adds that the pleasures of mind, of sight, and of hearing are beautiful because, of all pleasures, they are in the highest degree innocuous and excellent.

If you understand excellent to be the same as profitable, the previous uncertainty will raise its head again. The profitable makes the good and is thus the cause of the good. Cause and effect are different. Therefore the profitable is different from the good. From this it follows that the beautiful is different from the good. And so the beautiful is not good, and the good is not the beautiful.

But, as I have said, if you show them to be excellent, that is, innocuous, easy, full of air and life and light, you will gain mastery of what is true. For beauty is nothing other than the splendour of the highest good, shining in those things which are perceived by eyes, ears, and mind, and by means of them turning sight, hearing, and mind towards the Good itself. From this it comes about that beauty is a circle of divine light, emanating from the Good, abiding in the Good, and forever turned back towards the Good by means of the Good. This mystery, which Socrates declares he learnt from Diotima the sibyl, he revealed to his followers, but not to the Sophists.

What is the Good itself, the one principle of all creation, the pure impulse which imparts life to all that follows? What is Beauty itself? It is the life-giving impulse flowing from the primal fount of all good things; firstly, imparting unending adornment to the divine mind with the hierarchy of Ideas; then filling the subsequent divine beings and minds with a series of principles; thirdly, embellishing souls with numerous discourses; fourthly, embellishing natures with seeds; and fifthly, adorning matter with forms.

It certainly creates visible bodies and the eyes that see them. It infuses a clear spirit into the eyes to enable them to see. It paints the bodies with colours to enable them to be seen. But the ray of the eyes and the colours of the bodies are not enough to produce sight without the presence of the one Light itself, which is above the many and by which many specific lights have been bestowed on eyes and bodies: the Light which illuminates, arouses, and strengthens.

In the same way, the first impulse itself, which is God, has bestowed beauty and activity upon individual beings through the act of creation.

Of course, when this activity has been implanted in the passive object, it is weak and incapable of going into operation.

But the one everlasting and invisible light of the divine Sun is present in all things, gives warmth and life to all things, and arouses, fulfils, and strengthens all things. This divine Sun Orpheus describes as 'cherishing all and bearing itself aloft above all'.

As the impulse and strength of all, it is called the Good. As the life-giver, healer, assuager, and awakener, it is called the Beautiful. As the focus, within cognisable objects, of those three powers of the conscious soul, it is known as Beauty. As the link between the power to cognise and that which is cognised, it is Truth.

As the Good, it creates, regulates, and fulfils. As the Beautiful, it illuminates and imparts grace. Everything, however, needs to be pre-pared to receive the grace of the divine splendour. Bodies need propor-tion, which is based on arrangement and outward beauty. Sounds need harmony, which is composed of numbers and intervals. Duties need uprightness of living directed to a good end. Study needs ordering towards a true objective. The soul needs purity in order to turn from the lower to the higher. The mind needs insight to look upon the Good itself by means of the eternal.

With the help of all these the ray of divine beauty gradually penetrates. In relation to the body, it shines in measured uniformity, subject to place and movement. In relation to sounds, it shines in harmony, beyond the limits of place but scattered by movement. In relation to duties and study and the soul, it shines in movement but is established on a living principle. In relation to the mind, it shines above movement and in an eternal succession of Ideas. In relation to the Good itself, it shines as pure activity, bearing life and grace to all.

I beg you, Piero de' Medici, pre-eminent among all men as you are, to read these words with your usual diligence; for you will certainly perceive the surpassing beauty of your mind and you will observe how close you have come to the subject of our discussion, which is Beauty itself.

Plato's *Lysis*
or *Concerning Friendship:*
Summary Dedicated to Piero de' Medici,
Father of His People

WHEN SOCRATES holds discussions with the Sophists and their followers, he refutes false opinions; but rather than teach true opinions he merely hints at them. For when the false have been refuted, then keen minds hunt out the true on a faint trail.

This is evident in *Euthydemus, Protagoras, Meno, Hippias, Euthyphro,* and *Lysis.* But when he converses with his own pupils and students, he reveals and teaches what is merely inferred from many of the dialogues. And so, since in *Lysis* the discussion about friendship takes place among the disciples of the Sophists, Socrates is concerned more with refuting the false than with demonstrating the true. From this book we can infer Plato's view of friendship and love, but from the books of the *Laws* and from many others we can gather it more fully.

He defines friendship as an honourable communion of everlasting will. Its end is one life, its beginning is kinship, and its middle is love. By saying 'honourable' he excludes the associations of depraved men and the couplings of the licentious. By 'everlasting' he maintains that the fickle affections of young people, even though they be honourable, are not yet worthy to be called friendships. By 'will' he shows that no similarity of opinion or conduct is enough to give rise to friendship. By 'communion' he indicates the variable nature of affection. The end of communion is that one mind arises from two by will, one life from one will, and lastly from one life the fulfilment of one godhead and its principle.

The beginning by which the desire for this communion is aroused is kinship. Kinship means an affinity in principle, in star, and in being, as well as a measure of affection in soul and body; for those who depend on the One strive to return to the One, through the One, and towards the One.

30

The middle, which is like the pathway to friendship, is love. But since love is the desire for the beautiful, and since friendship is both drawn and declared equally by love, those who are going to be friends are of necessity beautiful.

I call those beautiful whose souls are beautiful. For man is soul. Man's body is an instrument, and whoever loves a beautiful body loves not the man but that which is of the man.

And so, as often as that kinship is present and is accompanied by beauty of soul, perfect friendship is born. If comeliness of body is added to this beauty of soul, they begin to love more quickly, and in a short time they attain the state of friendship.

This is what happened in the mutual affection between Plato and Dion.

But if comeliness of body is conjoined with deformity of soul, there arises a lust, not for honourable communion but for base coupling. From this proceeds not friendship, but firstly wantonness and then discord. For this reason, if kinship is lacking, they will never be friends.

If kinship is present, but all beauty is absent, they will occasionally be well-wishers rather than friends.

However, if beauty of body but not of soul is joined to kinship, there arises, instead of a desire for friendship, a passion for vile coupling.

When one is beautiful in soul and the other is base, this kinship begets an inclination to admonish and rebuke.

If the soul of one is beautiful and that of the other is neither beautiful nor base, the will to teach and the will to learn respectively issue forth from their kinship. At length, from that rebuking and from that teaching, friendship is born. This is indeed what Socrates' love for Phaedrus and Alcibiades demonstrates.

But when kinship finds beauty on both sides, it quickly begets indissoluble friendship. This holds true in the case of the affection between Plato and Aster.

And such is the view of our Plato on friendship, as gathered from many dialogues.

In the present dialogue, however, he firstly rebukes those who abuse love and gratify base lust under the guise of friendship. Then he admonishes those who consider themselves worthy of being loved simply for their comeliness of body. Thirdly, he refutes those whose view on friendship is less than true. Finally, he indicates to perceptive souls the narrow pathway for the pursuit of friendship.

The individual stages are plain to read in their respective places. For as Socrates mocks Hippothales and Ctesippus with irony and jests, he shows that they have been snared by base love. And as in their presence he instructs the youths in morals, he reminds lovers how to love and how to live at one.

And now that he has instructed the lovers, he enters upon the second part of the dialogue with the purpose of instructing the beloved. Here, in a long sequence of induction, he teaches that the proper way to catch friends is not with the shadowy form of this diminutive body, but with the real beauty of the soul, namely, wisdom and discretion.

In the third place he refutes, to begin with, the view of Solon, who says that loved ones are friends: on the contrary, they often hate their lovers. He adds that lovers are not friends either, for those who love are often regarded with hatred. At this point he concludes that mutual affection deserves to be called friendship.

Then he reprimands Empedocles, who has maintained that mere similarity of any kind is sufficient for friendship. Similarity in many fields of knowledge shows this to be false, for it spawns envy and hatred more often than it does friendship.

Under consideration soon afterwards is the view of Hesiod and Heraclitus that opposites are friends. He proves this to be false by the fact that, although hatred and love are opposites, they are not friends; nor are the just man and the unjust; and he gives other examples of this type.

If anything ever seems to seek out its opposite, as with dry and damp, hot and cold, it must be said not that it is loving its opposite, but that it is seeking from its opposite its own restoration. For if something uses heat over and above its own nature, it is restored to its natural equilibrium through coldness. And so it does not love coldness, but it loves the equilibrium attained through coldness. The same judgement may be made about all other opposites.

Now that these views have been refuted, Socrates, as if inspired, introduces another view as his own. He divides the feelings of the soul into three: the good soul, the bad, and the neutral. On account of their disparity, the bad is never a friend to the good. As a matter of justice, the bad is harmed by the bad, and so these two are not mutual friends. It is impossible also for the neutral to love the bad, for since the bad is obstructive, its very nature is always viewed with hatred.

The possibility remains that there is friendship between the good and the good, and between the neutral and the good. The first of these friendships is founded in joy, the second in desire. From these have arisen the two types of friendship.

But objections which seem to militate against this raise their heads. Socrates introduces them openly, but hints at their solutions in a secretive way.

The first objection is that the good is similar to the good, yet it was said in argument against Empedocles that similars are not friends. Here one must understand that it was not stated that similars are in no way friends, but it was denied that mere similarity of any kind was sufficient to beget friendship.

The second objection is this: the good is sufficient for itself, and so it does not desire any other, and so it does not love, and so it is not a friend of the good. Here one must explain that this absurdity does not follow from the mind of Plato, but from the words of Empedocles and Heraclitus, who do not distinguish between friendship and the desire for love and who therefore posit the necessity for everlasting desire to accompany friendship.

But Plato has it that friendship is a disposition derived from long-enduring love. This means that love is incipient friendship. But friendship is matured love, in which resides much more satisfaction than desire. From this it follows that anyone who has desired is already being satisfied. And so the disposition of friendship does not necessarily require the ardour of a present desire, but its satisfaction.

Therefore if the good desires the good less, none the less does the good rejoice in the good, because it has the greatest influence in preserving the reasonable basis of friendship. And this is the first type of friendship, namely, the friendship between the good and the good, a friendship based on joy rather than on desire.

And the second type is that which contains more desire than satisfaction: the friendship arising between the neutral and the good. How it is caused, on what account, and for what reason, is sufficiently clear from the text. He describes it firstly as opinion presents it, and then he makes improvements, one by one. For when he has said that the neutral loves the friendly good on account of the hostile bad and for the sake of the friendly good, he makes corrections at once by objecting to these statements.

Here he first teaches that all the friendships which concern men are imperfect, and that they are images of the friendship which reflects the first Good itself and the Author of all, who is loved first and who causes all these things to be loved.

33

And whoever loves anything has the First itself as the end of love. For from the first Good good is present in all; from the first beauty grace is present for everyone; but goodness draws us, while beauty entices. And so these lower things do not move us, but it is the First within them that draws and entices us. Therefore we love not these things but that which is simultaneously within them and outside. Here our Plato's devotion to God and his supreme piety shine forth with astonishing effect.

He further shows that we are not always friends because of another. For it is not on account of another good that we yearn for the first Good. Nor is it on account of the bad that you would desire the Good. For even if evil were removed from the scheme of things, the Good would remain dear by its own nature and it would draw the desires from that which is less good to a more befitting good.

For it is not the bad which arouses the appetite for the highest Good, but the insufficiency of the less good turns for its own satisfaction to the highest Good. This insufficiency should not be called the bad, because the bad never turns to the good, nor does one opposite turn to the other; but rather should it be called the incompleteness of the good.

Having raised these points of correction, he introduces a principle for investigating friendship more fully; for he says that kinship and affinity of nature beget friendship, and we spoke sufficiently about this at the beginning.

Lastly, he takes a bite at those youths and young men who do not know what is really worthy of love, or what true friendship is, or how it is produced in an honourable and steadfast way. Yet before they learn these things, they strive rashly, impudently, and impertinently to enter into friendship. But in order not to make them hostile to him, he hints at these things quietly and reproves himself along with them.

That is enough on the theme. Let us address ourselves to *Lysis*.

Summary of Plato's *Theaetetus*, a Work on Knowledge, Dedicated to Piero de' Medici, Father of His People

T HE DIALOGUE on knowledge soars aloft and raises questions worthy of the extraordinary perceptiveness of your mind, my Piero de' Medici. In this summary you will find a brief account of the salient points and their resolution. You will find a discussion of what knowledge is not, what it is, and whence and how it arises.

Socrates, for his part, asks what knowledge is, and Theaetetus replies that knowledge is geometry, arithmetic, and other disciplines of this kind, as well as the individual arts. Socrates will not accept this reply because it does not match the question. For the question was 'What is knowledge?' and Theaetetus does not say what it is, but enumerates the branches of knowledge and expounds what the branches of knowledge pertain to. For when we say 'Arithmetic', we are referring not to knowledge itself but to the knowledge of counting; and when we say 'Geometry', we mean the knowledge of measuring.

And so the answer cannot be taken seriously, since it is related to unknown factors. For no one can know what this knowledge of numbers or shapes is unless he knows what knowledge is. The reply is also long-winded: for although he could embrace the principle of knowledge in a small number of words, he embarks on a never-ending journey through lists of individual items.

Then he introduces the definition given by Protagoras, who says that knowledge is sense. Indeed, Protagoras considers man to be the measure of all things: of things that exist as 'are', and of things that do not exist as 'are not'; and however anything appears to anyone, that is how it is. For, he says, all things are as they are perceived through the senses; those which are perceived as imaginings are therefore perceived by an inner sense. Thus he would have it that knowledge is sense.

Indeed, on this point agree Thales of Miletus, Homer, Epicharmus,

Empedocles, Heraclitus, and Protagoras. For when Thales says that water is the beginning of all things, and when Homer says that Oceanus is the father of all and that Tethys is the mother of all, they are showing that all things are based on fluid.

The others we have mentioned express this by saying that nothing ever *is*, but that every single thing is continually becoming. Thus nothing is absolutely *this*, rather than absolutely *that*, but by means of movement, admixture and the relationship of one to another, it becomes and appears in one way to one and in another way to another.

That all things are in movement is clear, they believe, from the fact that all things are made by movement; and that all things are made by movement they infer to be true from the fact that whatever is made is maintained by that which makes it. Now those things pertaining to the soul, as well as those pertaining to the body, are maintained by movement and exercise, and perish through inactivity and sluggishness. Thus all things arise from movement.

Moreover, as long as the spheres of the heavens are in movement, the four elements remain mixed together. The more the elements are mixed together, the greater the number of lower beings that are born; and after these have been born, they are maintained by activity. Thus movement produces all these things.

They say, in addition, that generation arises from heat, and that heat arises from the movement of the sun or from the mutual impact of bodies. However, the fact that nothing of itself is a unity they infer from the following example: whiteness – or any other colour – is neither the sense of sight nor the movement of bodies but is a vibration occurring between sight and movement, that is, some phenomenon related to the eyes; and according to the changing dispositions of the beholder and the varying ways of beholding, different colours are seen and produced.

Moreover, the varying movement of the light-rays, striking against bodies and hitting the eyes, presents varied images of all kinds. Indeed, the colour of an object often appears different to different men and animals, and the colour of a specific object frequently appears different to the same person at different times, according to change in the actual nature of the object.

It is thought, therefore, that all that exists is movement, but that there are two kinds of movement: one in doing and the other in suffering the action. Through the interaction of these movements all things, they say, are produced.

Phenomena, though infinite in number, are of two kinds: the perceptible and the organs of perception, which always appear with the perceptible and accompany the perceptible. For whenever any power of perception and anything that is compatible with that power are united, two kinds of things arise from their union: in relation to the object there is the type that is to be perceived, as well as the colour, the taste, the smell, and so on; and in relation to the power of the soul there are the organs of perception.

When they are separated, such things do not occur, with the result that, of all that is presented to the five senses, there is nothing that has a specific nature; but objects that unite with the senses appear in different ways at different times. For nothing that acts or suffers exists in its own right but is in one type of union or the other. For this reason nothing is a unity of itself, but everything always comes into being in relation to something else and for the sake of something else. It never *is*, but is in a state of continual flux.

Socrates, however, refutes these statements by adducing the evidence that people who are drunk, delirious, insane, or asleep but dreaming, as well as people whose senses are impaired by some disease, declare that they perceive and contemplate things that are real and true, although we may say that all their perceptions are erroneous. Thus it comes about that the things which are seen are not all true.

Into the same doubtful category fall all those things that we say we perceive when we are awake and sober. For we divide our time almost equally between sleeping and waking. And so it is doubtful whether waking perceptions are truer or less dream-like than sleeping perceptions.

Those who hold that all phenomena are true to the one who is making the judgement would undoubtedly reply that because the different dispositions of those who are performing the action or those who are suffering the action give rise to different effects, and because the objects which are perceived act according to the disposition of the receiving sense-organ, perceptions are different in the wakeful person, the sleeper, the sick, and the healthy. For this reason the different judgements that are made are all true, because they appear to each perceiver as they are described.

For what was said earlier needs to be remembered: nothing is by nature absolutely one, but everything is related to something other, is for something other, and belongs to something other. Indeed, whatever comes into being *becomes* something, but nothing actually *is*. These views are therefore in harmony with each other.

According to Homer and Heraclitus, all things are in flux. According to Protagoras, man is the measure of all things. According to Theaetetus, knowledge is sense-perception. Against these men Socrates reasons as follows: If sense-perception be knowledge, then animals, having keener senses than man, will excel in knowledge. Again, if whatever is seen is true, then the thoughts of each and every man will be equally correct, and no man will be wiser than another, and God will be no wiser than man.

Moreover, the power of teaching, discussing, and refuting will be rendered void, since there will be nothing to be learned by people who make true judgements about everything and nothing to be sought by people who possess everything; and there will be nothing to be refuted, since all thought whatsoever will be true.

Furthermore, if sensing, such as seeing and hearing, is the same as knowing, then as soon as children devoid of learning look at some writing they see it and therefore know it. Conversely, if they be said not to know, they can also be said not to see. And as soon as we hear foreigners uttering their language, we, though previously unacquainted with their tongue, shall affirm what they are saying, for to hear is to know; and anyone who says he cannot understand is also saying that he cannot hear.

To this last point Protagoras will reply that we know what we see or hear and that we do not even perceive what we do not know; in the writing the children see shape and colour and the arrangement of the parts, and as they see so they know; listening to foreign words, they soon hear the high and the low sounds, and as they hear so they know. However, since they do not perceive the meanings of the writing or of the spoken words, they have no knowledge of them.

Against Protagoras the following is adduced:

'It follows from this, Protagoras, that when they know the meanings they will know them from something other than the senses. Knowledge is therefore different from the senses. Again, if seeing is knowing, then non-seeing will be non-knowing. But what someone sees and learns and remembers, he knows. Often, however, he does not see it and thus does not know it; and this means that he knows something and simultaneously does not know it. Besides, if you see something with one eye, you will see nothing with the closed eye, and thus you will see it and, equally, not see it. And so some contentious person might say: "If seeing is knowing, and non-seeing is non-knowing, then you know something and at the same time you know it not. Furthermore, when you view something from afar and in confusion, you certainly see, but you do not know, for you are in doubt. Therefore knowledge is not sense-perception.'"

Protagoras might reply that, first of all, a distinction needs to be made between memory and knowledge. For as soon as someone receives a sense-impression, he begins to hold it in memory, and then he remembers even without receiving sense-impressions; when he receives the same sense-impression again, then he recollects.

In the first situation he knows through action and not through habit; in the second he knows through habit and not through action; and in the third he knows through action and habit simultaneously. This is why, on occasions, he both knows and knows not.

But these are not contradictory conditions. For the way of knowing is not the same as the way of non-knowing. Therefore, when he sees not but remembers, he knows through habit and he knows not through action. But these are not mutually opposing conditions.

And when Socrates is said to be wiser than any other, Protagoras replies that people are not to be called wise because their judgements are true, or unwise because their judgements are false; for everyone judges that the impressions which he receives are received from things which move; that these things are moved by those which act; that the things which act are the things which are; and that the things which are are true and real.

From this he concludes that all make judgements which are true, but not everyone makes judgements which are good and honourable. He asserts those to be wise who, being well disposed, accept as good whatever is offered. They believe it to be good for themselves, and as they think, so they are. He affirms those to be unwise who, being ill disposed, judge things to be evil, and the things they judge are evil for them.

Against the statement that all men make true judgements Socrates reasons as follows. It happens in every life and at every opportunity that we consider we make true judgements about ourselves in certain matters, and true judgements about others in a few matters, for each reveals a particular ability but yields to another in an unfamiliar skill. Such a consideration is either true or false.

In either case, it follows that not all men think truly. For if this consideration of ours be true, it will be true that where someone makes a true judgement on many matters our own views will be false. Thus we do not all have true views. If our consideration be false, then we are frequently deceived in this at any rate; and so not every opinion is true.

Indeed, it often happens that what one man holds true is abhorrent to the view held by everyone else; and so, what is true for that man appears false to the others. However, there will thus be more false views than true views, and those by whom false views are held will out-number those by whom true views are held. For others, rather than that man, are the measure of all things.

Again, the view of Protagoras that every opinion is true is a paradox and goes beyond the view of nearly everyone else, which means that almost all other people consider his opinion to be wrong. Thus, if every opinion is true, and if this general verdict is true, then Protagoras' own position, which holds all opinion to be true, is thereby considered false and is indeed false. For by speaking in this way he is admitting that his position is false. And if he has said that people are thinking wrong-ly when they recoil from his words, the same conclusion follows: not every opinion is true.

Besides, the person who does not know – because he does not know the measure of that thing – cannot be. He who doubts knows not. All men doubt, and so there are many things they do not know. Not all men, therefore, are the measure of all things. And when he says that individual things are as they appear to individual people, he is mis-taken. For those aspects of the art of medicine which appear to the ignorant as healthy for the body or as harmful to the body are not always so. Opinion often deceives such people. Likewise, the factors which citizens in their deliberations discern as useful or harmful in the administration of the State are not necessarily so. For many of the things which they hope will be beneficial to us are, in fact, obstacles; and many of the things which they think will be harmful are actually beneficial.

If those things which are healthy and useful are not only established by the opinion and tradition of men, but also have some substance of their own, much more will that be true of that which is honourable and good. The good, indeed, is the beginning and the end of all that is useful.

For this reason, both in those matters concerning the care of the body and in those related to the soul and to the government of the State, things are not as they appear to any particular person. And indeed, if things were as they seem, then every time someone spoke of the future he would certainly be predicting it; and this is clearly not the case, for rarely do things turn out as it is believed they will.

Although people judge the future, it is not everyone who does so correctly; but it is the craftsman who can judge of those things that pertain to his art. The doctor rather than the musician foresees when there will be fever, and the musician rather than the doctor can see when there will be harmony.

Now that such points have been finally settled, Socrates takes the opportunity of speaking about freedom or bondage, and he discusses the freedom of those who practise philosophy and the bondage of citizens and orators; the quality of their respective lives; the aim of the philosopher, which is to rise from human ills to good things supernal; the rewards awaiting those who seek the heavenly realm; and the pains awaiting those who drink their fill of earthly things.

After making this digression, he returns to the matter in hand, the basis of which was the view of Heraclitus that all things are in movement. The opposite was held by Parmenides, Melissus, and Zeno of Elea, who posited that all is one and unmoving. It is their teaching that Plato expounds and approves of in his book *On the single principle of all things*, which we have translated.

In contradistinction to Heraclitus and Protagoras, he begins his discussion with the division of movement. There are two kinds of movement. The first is movement in relation to place, and the second is movement in relation to the nature of the thing. The first is called bearing, and the second is called change.

There are two types of bearing: transverse and circular. For a movement is either from one place to another or around one and the same place.

But movement accomplished within the very nature of the thing that is moved is either in accordance with its substance or in relation to its quantity or quality. If it is in accordance with the substance related to the very being that is moved, it is generation. If it is related to non-being, it is degeneration. If it accords with greater quantity, it is called increase; and if it accords with less, it is called decrease.

Movement from one quality to another is called disposition. Then different names are assigned to different qualities: calefaction describes heat; frigefaction describes cold; coloration describes colour; and so on.

Once this differentiation has been introduced, Socrates asks if all things are severally moved by these two kinds of movement, or if many things are moved by one kind of movement, while others are moved by both kinds.

If many things are moved by one kind of movement, it follows that they are stationary no less than in movement. For if they are moved in a particular way, they are also at rest in a particular way. The view of those philosophers does not accept this, however, but states that all things, in all circumstances, move without any rest, which means that they are kept in motion by both types of movement. Thus, while things are being transferred from one place to another, they are at the same time moving unceasingly from one disposition to another: from heat to cold, from whiteness to blackness, and conversely.

The question is whether or not they remain briefly in one of these forms. If they do remain, it follows that not all the states of rest are debarred. If they do not remain, then even while something is being described as hot or white it ceases to be so. In fact, the form ceases to exist even before the description has started. Hence nothing is ever truly described or perceived, and it cannot be said that something is hot rather than non-hot, or white rather than non-white, since it abides in nothing and both is and is not while it is being manifested. For this reason the forms of things are unknown to us.

The same is true for the senses. For sight does not endure for a moment within the sense of sight, and hearing does not endure for a moment within the sense of hearing. Thus, even while we are asserting that we are seeing and hearing, the fact is that we are not-seeing and not-hearing as much as seeing and hearing. Hence it follows that, when the senses have been removed and when the reality of the senses has been removed, it is impossible to say that knowledge of the senses exists.

He then adds another reason, which needs to be understood: Plato does not attribute to the body any consciousness or life. That which is alive perceives. The soul is alive, and the soul perceives. Within the body neither life nor sense is affirmed, but the operations of life and sense are affirmed.

This is why Plato wishes to describe as the five organs of sense what others call the five senses; and he considers that nothing is perceived by these instruments, but that through them, as if through channels, individual things are perceived by a single power of the soul which he calls the common sense and into which the various percepts flow from all directions through the separate organs of the body, like lines from the circumference to the centre of the circle: colours through the eyes; sounds through the ears; scents through the nostrils; flavours through the tongue; and through the whole body warmth and coldness and whatever is wet or dry, heavy or light, soft or hard, smooth or rough, rarefied or dense, sharp or blunt.

It is clear that the soul perceives with a single force rather than with many forces, because when perceiving colour we do not say it is sound, and when perceiving taste we do not declare it to be fragrance. A person cannot distinguish one thing from another unless he knows both. No organ can reach what another organ can; and even if it could do so, it would do so in a different way.

And so the differences among things that are perceived lie not in the organs of perception, but in a single power of the soul to perceive individual items and, at the same time, distinguish one from another. Since this power can do all this unaided, which even the Aristotelians do not deny, where is the need for many senses? This sense which they call the common sense is inherent in all creatures as soon as they are born.

Apart from this there is another power, which he calls imagination, opinion, and cognition. The function of this power is to judge of those things which the common sense perceives through the five organs: what they are, as well as of what kind; which of them is the same as itself and different from another; which is in isolation, and which two or three are united; which are similar and which dissimilar; good or bad; beautiful or base; useful or harmful.

Its function is also to move from one thing to another by the process of reasoning; to connect one thing with another; and to compare things past and future with things present.

And so it is by this power that we judge unity and number; the same and the different; similarity and dissimilarity; the beautiful and the base; the good and the evil; the useful and the useless. It is evident that this judgement is not present in creatures as soon as they are born, but much later; and it is not present in all creatures but only in some, for we perceive these things with a force other than common sense. This power he calls perfect imagination and opinion.

But even this power is not enough, for it judges all these things in its own particular way, at particular times, and in particular places and circumstances. Yet we know that we judge of the same matters as a whole and in a general way: not why this man is here now, or why this useful thing is where it is, but why humanity itself always exists and why there is usefulness in all places.

For this reason another power is needed, which, while perceiving generally the universal principles of creation, will also proceed from one principle to another and will reason as it does so. No one doubts that this is what happens within us when we join one syllogism to another. We call this reasoning process or consideration universal, for we call opinion itself a particular process of reasoning and consideration.

Finally, this process is confirmed by mind, which perceives all the principles of nature not by discursive reasoning but by simple steadfast observation, for above movement and time there must be stillness and eternity: movement and time within reason, but stillness and eternity within mind. For mind does not learn one thing after another but apprehends everything at once.

Above mind there is the unity of the soul – the mark of the highest Good – which is linked, not to the principles and Ideas of creation, but to the first principle of all things, the One itself.

Since all the powers of the soul which depend on consciousness have been enumerated, and since knowledge resides in consciousness, in which force there is knowledge above all, it is not compatible with sense, as it has now taken up its position with many principles, and especially as the common sense does not judge the essences of things but merely perceives some bodily phenomena. Whoever knows not essence knows not truth. Whoever is devoid of truth is far removed from knowledge.

Knowledge, therefore, is not within the realm of sense, where the soul does not perceive of itself, but perceives by means of the body and is for that reason often deceived. But perhaps knowledge resides in the realm of imagination and opinion, where we can now perceive essences and where the soul makes judgements by itself and without the operations of the body.

Secondly, this view is agreeable to Theaetetus: that knowledge is opinion; not any opinion, but true opinion, for false opinion is ignorance. But since Theaetetus has divided opinion into two – the true and the false – Socrates immediately asks how there can be false opinion, and he posits a situation where someone believes what he knows to be either what he knows or what he does not know.

And so he reasons as follows: A man who conjectures what is untrue never does so through thinking that there are some things which he knows and other things which he also knows. For if he knows two things he never mistakes one for the other. And he never mistakes things which he does not know for other things which he does not know. For he cannot make any judgement about things that have never entered his consciousness.

And he never thinks that what he knows is what he does not know or that what he does not know is what he knows. For who would mistake the known for the unknown, or the unknown for the known?

It thus seems impossible for anyone to conjecture in these ways that which is untrue. But perhaps people make such conjectures in some other way, when they conjecture those things which are not. In this case, false opinion would be to conjecture the things which are not.

But this, too, is impossible. For anyone who sees sees some one; anyone who sees some one sees something that exists; while anyone who sees what does not exist does not see some one; anyone who does not see some one sees nothing; and anyone who sees nothing does not see at all. Therefore, either he sees not or he sees what is. We can make similar affirmations with regard to hearing and the other senses.

For these reasons, since conjecture follows sense, anyone who conjectures will conjecture some one; anyone who conjectures some one conjectures something that exists and thus conjectures that which is; while anyone who conjectures what does not exist does not conjecture some one at all; if not some one, then nothing; if he conjectures nothing, he does not conjecture at all. Therefore, either he does not conjecture at all, or he conjectures that which is. Thus no one can conjecture, in this way either, that which is untrue, for he would be conjecturing things which are not.

There is another way in which we might make the mistake of taking one thing for another: of mistaking the base for the beautiful, and the useless for the useful. This, too, Socrates refutes in the following manner: To conjecture is to talk to oneself: we ask ourselves questions, we reply, we affirm, and we deny. This inner conversation is no worse than outer conversation, but in outer conversation no one ever says that base is beautiful, that man is ox, that like is unlike, and things of this kind.

Far less, therefore, will he assert in his considerations that one of these is something. For either he knows both or he knows only one of them. If he knows both, he would never confuse the two; if he knows one, the same applies, for he would never mistake what he knows for something that has not yet entered his consciousness.

The conclusion is that no way seems to have been yet discovered whereby false opinion can take its abode within us.

In this dialogue, as in the *Philebus*, *Sophist*, and *Meno*, Plato uses six names pertaining to the power of the soul, in order to denote its six functions. For, subsequent to the common sense, when the soul,

45

which also perceives the common senses, perceives by the power of conjecture, this first perception is called imagination. As it retains what has been apprehended, it is called memory. As it takes up once more what it has preserved, it is called reminiscence. When it takes up one thing after another, as if it were going through a process of reasoning, it is called cogitation. When this process is completed, and something is affirmed or denied, it is called opinion. When opinion has been perceived through sense and memory, and when soul, re-fashioning, looks back upon these things from which the others have emanated and believes the things that are images to be real things, Plato calls this a kind of picture and phantasy.

And when he introduces the image of the block of wax, he is certainly not referring to the nature of the brain, for he said that the block of wax was not in the body but in the soul. But since there is nothing corporeal within the incorporeal, these things are to be understood not literally but by transference and similarity of operation.

He does not mean that the images of things are fixed in the body or are represented in the soul by external objects, but that the soul holds them through its own nature, or that, once the soul has taken leave of the external movements and passions of the body, it conceives forms and principles through its own power. Anyone who entertains doubts on these matters should read the commentaries of Plotinus, the greatest of the commentators.

Now that these points have been expounded, it is time to go back to the different kinds of false opinion. Socrates refers to a great number and rejects many of them; and as a way of curbing the arrogance of the Sophists he repeatedly refutes the things which they accept.

In brief, we can gather from Plato's way of thinking that when something perceptible to the senses first impinges upon us, and by its contact a sense-impression and a memory are formed within us, and later the same experience happens to us again, we link the previous memory with the subsequent sense-impression, and we then say 'Socrates', 'horse', 'fire', and so on. This is called an opinion, when we link a previous memory with a subsequent sense-impression.

And whenever the things being joined are in harmony there is true opinion; if they are not in harmony there is false opinion. For if someone who has the form of Socrates in his memory lights upon Plato and thinks that, through some similarity, he is meeting Socrates once more, and if he then, taking in the impression of Plato as if from Socrates, makes it fit the memory of Socrates, the result is false opinion.

And in this way false opinion arises from the linking of the sense-impression with thought. It also arises through linking and exchanging the thought of one thing with the thought of something else, for just by thinking and without sense-impressions anyone can confuse the forms of certain numbers, as when xii is mistaken for xi or, conversly, xi for xii.

But a doubt arises here. For anyone who holds appearances knows those things whose appearance he holds and therefore knows these numbers. But if he confuses them, he does not know them. Thus he both knows them and knows them not, simultaneously. The answer to be given is that this is not absurd, for a man who knows in one way may be ignorant in a different way: he knows by habit, but he knows not in action. For this reason these points present no difficulty; and the two kinds of false opinion were identified and explained a little while ago.

Another doubt now arises: if a man who knows two things holds a false opinion through mistaking them, taking one to be the other, he seems not to know the very thing of which he has knowledge and, what is worse, not to know through knowledge rather than through ignorance; for knowledge is the cause of the mistake, while the mistake is the cause of ignorance. For if it is that knowledge makes us not to know, there is nothing to prevent ignorance from making us know.

To this Theaetetus replies that the form of ignorance, as well as the form of knowledge, is to be posited within the soul, and that the man who mistakes one thing for another is deceived and does not know through ignorance rather than through knowledge. This reply is far from satisfactory, for the question will be asked just as it was earlier: If he mistakes those forms one for the other, does he know both or not know both, or does he know one but not the other? And from this the whole of the previous debate will arise once more.

Again, if the forms to be posited are known partly through knowledge and partly through ignorance, other forms need to be posited by which these forms are known; and then further forms are needed by which those forms may be known; and so on *ad infinitum.*

A new answer is required to meet this case. For, as Socrates had indicated earlier, it should be said that the concepts of things are not the causes of the mistake: the causes of the mistake are the mixing of concepts, perpetual neglect, and an external similarity that has not been closely examined.

47

It therefore seems that our ignorance is due not to knowledge but to confusion, neglect, and illusion, although these things cannot be judged absolutely before a definition of knowledge has been given. For we discern darkness through light, silence through sound, evil through good, false through true. It seems, therefore, that knowledge needs to be defined before an exposition of false opinion can be made, if we wish to gain a perfect understanding of false opinion.

This is why Theaetetus declares knowledge to be true opinion. Socrates rejects this definition on the grounds that the art of oratory persuades but does not teach; the man who persuades brings in opinion, and when he relates the truth he brings in true opinion, but not knowledge. For nowhere is there definite knowledge about those things which are always in movement and which behave differently at different times. Such are the human affairs of which the orators speak, especially when they persuade their hearers to believe things which they themselves doubt and have never witnessed.

Then Theaetetus adds the definition given by Leucippus and Theodorus of Cyrene: Knowledge is true opinion conjoined with reason; and therefore those things that have reason can be known, while those lacking reason cannot be known. And Prodicus of Cos, following Leucippus, maintained that the elements of creation, being simple and thus without reason, are unknown, while compounds, which may possess reason, are known.

They understand reason, or definition, to be a form of words proclaiming the substance and property of the thing in question. Since this includes a number of items – a subject, a predicate, and a connective, these being a verb and nouns – it indicates a compound; but an element, being simple and therefore devoid of reason, remains unknown.

Socrates refutes both these statements, beginning with the second statement that elements, being simple, are unknown, while the things that are produced from these elements, being composite, are known. Then he refutes the earlier statement that knowledge is true opinion conjoined with reason.

And, for the sake of example, he takes the letters as the elements, and the syllable as the compound; but he intends his treatment of these to be applicable to everything. The first counter-argument is that just as compounds depend on elements, so the knowledge of compounds is perfected by the knowledge of their elements; for nothing that has a cause can be known in isolation from its cause. It is thus impossible to know compounds if their elements are unknown.

Again, take any compound: for example, **S-O**, the first syllable of Socrates' name. Is this syllable two elements, or is it something that has taken its birth from the conjoining of elements?

If the former, then anyone who knows this syllable **S-O** knows its two elements, and on being asked 'What is **S-**O?' will answer '**S** and **O**.' And if he does not know **S** and **O** he will never know **S-O**. For if he does not know one of them he cannot know them both. It is therefore impossible to know compounds if their elements are unknown.

But perhaps someone will say that the syllable exists as a form in its own right, not as elements but as something beyond them. To him Socrates puts this question: Does this form, this syllable, have parts or not? If it has parts, it is a totality, a whole. But a totality, a whole, is nothing but all its parts, because it is susceptible to numbers, and the whole number is nothing but the sum of all the unities that it contains, and thus this form will consist of parts, and the parts, by virtue of being parts, will be of the whole.

Therefore, just as the form is known, so are its elements known. For if one knows the form, one knows the totality, the whole. If one knows the totality, the whole, one knows that none of its parts is missing. One therefore knows that it has individual parts, and thus one knows those individual parts, not knowing which one could not know whether or not they were all present. It is therefore impossible to know the form without knowing its elements.

But if someone says that a single form has no parts, on the ground that the elements of which it consists are not its parts, it follows that it is simple and indivisible: for this reason, just as an element, being simple, was said to be unknown, so the form itself, being simple, is said to be unknown; and thus, if the elements are unknown, there is no way in which the forms which are made of these elements can be known. From this it is also patently obvious that because in all arts the basis of each art needs to be understood, the elements of those things treated of by that art need to be understood. Otherwise all work is to no effect.

Once this point has finally been refuted, Socrates now begins to argue against the main thrust of the proposition, where it was stated that knowledge is true opinion conjoined with reason. For three things can be meant by the word 'reason': reason itself; a consideration of the elements of a thing; a definition.

If the first is meant, then every opinion will be knowledge. For whether our opinion be true or false, we have the power to utter what we feel, and therefore even a man forming a false opinion will form it with reason.

If the second meaning is taken, a man will be said to 'know' whenever he considers the elements. But this is not the case, for by considering the elements one can make transpositions and change the order and relate the element of one thing to another thing and match the element of the second thing to the first. Anyone who has confused these things cannot be said to know.

If one understands the third meaning, that of definition, and calls knowledge true opinion conjoined with definition, our counter-argument is as follows: A definition is a recognition of difference; and so anyone who is making a definition is assigning a difference to something, in addition to what it has in common with other things. But if someone really has a view of Socrates and Theaetetus, does he, by holding that view, perceive the differences between Socrates and Theaetetus, or not? If he does not perceive differences, he does not really have a view, for I would never really distinguish one from the other if I did not discern the distinguishing features of each. Therefore, the very fact that one actually has a view means that one understands differences. And so, to true opinion there is no need to add 'reason', the concept of difference.

But perhaps someone will say that within opinion itself there should be included some sense and concept of difference rather than the definite understanding of natural difference, and thus to the definition of knowledge should be added the understanding of difference. Against such a person Socrates reasons as follows: It is an absurd definition which defines something in terms of itself. But when we say that knowledge is true opinion conjoined with reason, that is, conjoined with the understanding of difference, we are defining knowledge in terms of knowledge. For the understanding of difference is the knowledge of difference; and thus knowledge will be true opinion conjoined with the knowledge of difference, which is a ridiculous thing to say.

On the basis of all these considerations the false definitions given by the Sophists have now been refuted: the first, which said that knowledge is equivalent to the individual functions that are learnt; the second, that knowledge is sense; the third, that knowledge is true opinion; the fourth, that knowledge is true opinion conjoined with explanatory words; the fifth, that it is true opinion combined with a consideration of elements; the sixth, that it is true opinion combined with the imagination of difference; and the seventh, that it is true opinion conjoined with the knowledge of difference.

Now that all these have at last been refuted, it is time to see what Plato teaches. In the sixth book of the *Republic* he follows two Pythagoreans, Brontinus and Archytas, in positing two kinds of things: the intelligible and the perceptible. The intelligible is steadfast and incorporeal, while the perceptible is changeable and corporeal. The way to a knowledge of the intelligible he calls reason; the way to the perceptible he calls sense. The general comprehension of the intelligible he calls intelligence; the general comprehension of the perceptible he calls opinion.

But he divides each kind into two. For his view is that there are the first intelligible and the second intelligible. In the first intelligible are contained Ideas, which are the forms and concepts of the divine mind, together with the other minds and the souls. In the second intelligible are numbers and shapes. Although numbers and shapes are incorporeal, they are subject to some division and thus are not to be considered to rank in dignity with indivisible substances. Awareness of Ideas he calls intellect, but he describes awareness of numbers and shapes as intellectual cogitation.

The perceptible is also divided into two. In the first perceptible he locates all bodies and things bodily. In the second he locates the shadows and reflections of bodies, whether they appear in water or in other reflective surfaces; and he considers that they are to bodies as numbers are to things divine. Perception of bodies he calls belief; perception of shadows he calls imagination.

Then he says that there is no knowledge in relation to the shadows of bodies, bodies themselves, or numbers; but he locates knowledge only in the realisation of things divine. This is what he meant at the beginning of this dialogue when he proposed that knowledge and wisdom are identical. For he proclaims at all times that wisdom is contemplation of the divine.

That intellect, or knowledge, differs from opinion he demonstrates in his book *On Nature*, in the following way: If intellect and true opinion are two, then Ideas as such must be grasped by intellect rather than by sense. But if, as some believe, true opinion differs no whit from intellect, then all the physical things which we perceive must be taken as certain. But I believe that they are to be considered as two, for there is a great gulf between them: in fact, it is instruction which makes one of them known to us, but it is the acceptance of persuasion which makes the other known; one always with true principle, but the other without any principle; one immoveable by any cause, the other wavering and uncertain.

Does every man have a share of right opinion? Does intellect belong to God and to a very small band of chosen men? Plato makes the same points in *Meno* and *Philebus*.

What, then, is knowledge? It is the understanding of things divine by infallible reason. It is within intellect firstly and for ever; it is within reason secondly, but not for ever. For, since reason is midway between intellect and opinion, it becomes filled with the errors of opinion whenever it moves towards the lower realm and ceases to contemplate the divine. But when it turns to mind, which is its guide, it imbibes the consciousness of the divine: this Plato calls wisdom when it is in mind, and he calls it recollection when it is in reason.

And so in this dialogue he has discussed the midwife's skill, by which we recollect, so that we may understand not only what knowledge is but also how it is acquired. Where it comes from, and through whom, he explained when he said that Socrates performed the office of midwife at God's command.

Knowledge is therefore the understanding of things divine by infallible reason. It abides in mind and flows forth into reason. It is put into mind by God, and it is brought to reason by a teacher of dialectic under the grace of God. It guides reason into mind and unites mind with divinity.

Summary of Plato's *Ion*
or *On Poetic Frenzy*,
Dedicated to the Magnanimous
Lorenzo de' Medici

MY EXCELLENT Lorenzo, our Plato in the *Phaedrus* defines frenzy as a dissociation of the mind.

He gives two kinds of dissociation: one arising from human diseases, the other from God. He calls the first one madness, and the second one he calls divine frenzy. By madness man is cast down beneath the human condition, and from being a man he is to some extent rendered a brute. By divine frenzy he is lifted above the nature of man and passes into God.

Now divine frenzy is the illumination of the rational soul by which God draws the soul, which has fallen from the higher to the lower, back from the lower to the higher.

The fall of the soul to bodies, from the one principle of all things, is made through four levels: mind, reason, hypothesis, and nature. For since there are six levels in the total hierarchy of creation, the highest level being the One itself and the lowest the body, the four which we have just mentioned being intermediate, anything falling from the first to the last must fall through the four intermediate ones.

The One itself is the end and measure of all things and is devoid of both infinity and multiplicity. Mind is indeed multiplicity, but steadfast and eternal. Reason is multiplicity, moving yet finite. Hypothesis is multiplicity, moving and infinite, yet united by substance and points. Nature is the same, except that it is diffused through the points of the body. But the body is infinite multiplicity subject to movement and divided by substance, points, and moments.

To these our soul attends: through them it descends, and through them it ascends. For as it moves out from the One itself, which is the principle of all, it has obtained a certain unity which unifies its entire essence, its powers, and its actions: a unity from which and to which

"fall" = emanation in my Platonism article

the other things in the soul are related, just as the radii of a circle are related to and from the centre. Indeed, it unites not only the parts of the soul among themselves and to the whole soul, but also the whole soul to the One itself, the cause of all.

As the soul depends on the divine mind, it contemplates, through mind and by steadfast action, the Ideas of all things. As the soul attends to itself, it gathers together the universal principles of creation, and by reason it runs from principles to conclusions. As the soul attends to the body, it conceives and traverses, by hypothesis, the particular forms of moving things. As the soul reaches matter, it uses nature as an instrument to unite and move and shape matter, whence proceed generations and expansions, along with their opposites.

yes — opinion; doxa?

So you see that it falls from the One, which is above eternity, into eternal multiplicity; from eternity into time; from time into place and matter. For this reason, just as it descends through four levels, so it must needs ascend through four.

Now it is divine frenzy which brings about the turn towards the higher levels, as is maintained in Plato's definition.

remeatio

= priesthood

There are thus four kinds of divine frenzy: the first is poetic frenzy; the second, that of the Mysteries; the third, prophecy; the fourth, the movement of love. Now poetry is from the Muses, mystery from Dionysus, prophecy from Apollo, and love from Venus. Indeed, the soul cannot return to the One unless it itself be made one. But having been made many, it has fallen into a body: it has been split into various operations, and it attends to separate items.

The result is that its higher parts are almost falling asleep; the lower parts are lording it over the others; the higher parts are affected by drowsiness, the lower parts by agitation; and indeed the whole soul is filled with discord and cacophony. Therefore the task of poetic frenzy is firstly, through musical tones, to arouse those parts which slumber; through harmonious sweetness, to soothe those which are disturbed; and finally, through the harmonising of diverse elements, to dispel dissonant discord and temper the various parts of the soul.

Nor is this all: for multiplicity still remains in the soul. And so there is the Mystery, which with expiations and sacred rites and the whole worship of the gods directs the aim of all the parts of the mind, whereby God is worshipped. Thus, when the separate parts of the soul have been directed to the one mind, the soul has now been made wholly one from many.

Xty or theurgy?

Op 1281 – 1282

4 Frenzies
4 Furores one of Ficinos favorite
think.   topics for Allen on Phaedrus
           pp 58 - 62
ION

Then the task of the third frenzy is to lead the mind back to unity itself, the head of the soul. Apollo effects this through prophecy. For when the soul rises above the mind and into unity, it perceives the future.

Finally, when the soul has become one, I mean the one which is inherent in the very essence of the soul, it remains for it to be changed thereby into the One which is above essence. This is what heavenly Venus herself accomplishes through love, that is, through the desire for divine beauty and the yearning for the good.

And so the first frenzy tempers discord and dissonance; the second frenzy makes the tempered parts into one whole; the third frenzy takes the one whole above its parts; and the fourth frenzy leads to the One which is above essence and is absolute.

The first frenzy makes a distinction between the good horse, that is, reason and hypothesis, and the bad horse, that is, confused fantasy and nature. The second frenzy subjects the bad horse to the good, and it subjects the good horse to the charioteer, that is, to the mind. The third frenzy directs the charioteer towards his own master, that is, towards unity, the pinnacle of the mind. The fourth frenzy turns the master of the charioteer towards the master of all things, in whose presence the charioteer is happy and rests the horses near the manger, that is, near divine beauty, offering them ambrosia and then nectar to drink, that is, the vision of beauty and the joy from this vision.

These are the four operations of frenzy with which Plato deals generally in the *Phaedrus*; and he deals particularly with the last frenzy, which is love, in the *Symposium*, but with the first – poetic frenzy – in the present dialogue, which is entitled *Ion*.

In the *Phaedrus* he defines poetic frenzy as that possession by the Muses which, after selecting a gentle and invincible soul, arouses and excites it through lyrical and other poetry instructive to the human race. 'Possession' means the seizing of the soul and its turning towards the divine influences of the Muses. 'Gentle' means, as it were, mobile and conformable to the Muses; for unless it has been prepared, it is not possessed. 'Invincible', because after it has been seized, it overcomes all and it cannot be polluted or overcome by any of the lower things. 'It arouses': it recalls the soul from the sleep of the body to the wakefulness of the mind; from the darkness of ignorance to the light; from death to life; from the oblivion of Lethe to the memory of the divine. 'It excites': it stimulates and inspires the soul to express in song those things which it contemplates and foresees.

After this definition he adds that he who approaches the poetic temple of the Muses without frenzy is himself empty, and so is his poetry, as though poetry of any worth may not be obtained without the highest blessing of God. He maintains the same thing in *Ion* and expounds the origin of frenzy and the number of levels through which it descends.

Now in the fourth book of the *Laws* Plato says that God, fortune, and art govern all human affairs. From this it follows that poetry is the gift of God, the chance of fortune, or the work of art. Which of these it most truly is is the question which Socrates pursues with Ion the rhapsode. In this book 'rhapsode' means a reciter, an interpreter, and a singer of songs.

Ion interpreted the songs of Homer and sang them to the lyre before the people and was so moved that he expounded no poet other than Homer, not even a poet who spoke with the same ability as Homer. But all of Homer's words he would quickly expound. Hence the following reasoning: When Ion reveals what Homer writes, it may be by chance, by art, or by divine inspiration. It is not by chance, for if it were he would not interpret all of his words, but only a few, and those without continuity and order. It is not by art, because anyone who has an art in its entirety is able to judge whatever is subservient to that art. Of course, the poems of Hesiod and of others are subservient to the same art as are Homer's, and this is especially true of poems which deal with the same themes. Ion, however, gives no attention to these, although he expounds Homer perfectly. Therefore he does not judge by art. There remains the possibility that he judges by divine inspiration. From this it is clear that Ion, the Poet's interpreter, and many others who have been similarly affected, interpret the poetry of others by divine prompting.

Now as human ability is too weak to grasp poetry already transmitted, it is much weaker still at actually producing it. This is why neither Homer nor any other true poet pursued poetry without heavenly inspiration. Socrates demonstrates this here in other ways as well.

Firstly, like this: All poets transmit the arts and sciences, but they have all taught that it is impossible by human endeavour, since it is very difficult to grasp even part of a single one. They make their revelations, therefore, not by human skill but by divine prompting. The reasoning behind this is that after the onset of frenzy has abated, many poets largely fail to understand what they have written, although, in their frenzy, they have correctly discussed, in relation to specific arts, things which the craftsmen of those particular arts discern through a process of specialisation.

Moreover, we often see a simple, untrained man suddenly emerge as a good poet and sing something magnificent and divine. To achieve great things in an instant is not the work of human ability but of one divinely inspired. In this matter God shows clearly that this intelligence is imparted by His will. To prove that this is so, He often seizes upon the untrained rather than the refined, the mad rather than the prudent, lest, if He were to use perceptive and prudent men for these purposes, it would be thought that such purposes were achieved through human perception and toil. Therefore, since poetry is not from fortune and not from art, it is bestowed by God and by the Muses.

When he says 'God' he means Apollo; when he says 'Muses' he means the souls of the spheres of the world. Of course, Jupiter is the mind of God, from which comes Apollo, the mind of the world-soul and the soul of the whole world, together with the eight souls of the celestial spheres, those nine souls being called the nine Muses because as they move the heavens harmoniously they produce musical melody which, when distributed into nine sounds, namely, the eight notes of the spheres together with the one harmony of them all, gives rise to the nine Sirens singing to God.

Wherefore Apollo is led by Jupiter, and the Muses are led by Apollo, that is, the chorus of Muses is led by the mind of the world-soul, because just as that mind is illuminated by Jupiter, so does it illuminate the souls of the world and of the spheres.

Now the levels through which that frenzy descends are these: Jupiter seizes Apollo; Apollo gives light to the Muses; the Muses arouse and stir up the gentle but invincible souls of the poets; the poets, being inspired, inspire their own interpreters; the interpreters move the listeners.

Some souls are seized by some Muses and others by others, because some souls are allotted to some spheres and stars and others to others, as is maintained in the *Timaeus*. The Muse Calliope is the voice which arises from all the voices of the spheres. Urania is the voice of the starry heaven, so appointed by merit; Polyhymnia, the voice of Saturn, by reason of the memory of ancient things which Saturn displays, as well as a dry, cold temperament; Terpsichore, the voice of Jupiter, giver of health to the choir of men; Clio, the voice of Mars, by reason of the desire for glory; Melpomene, the voice of the Sun, because it is the moderator of the whole world; Erato, the voice of Venus, on account of love; Euterpe, the voice of Mercury, by reason of an honourable delight in weighty matters; Thalia, the voice of the Moon, on account of her evergreen quality bestowed upon things by moisture.

Apollo, moreover, is the soul of the Sun, and his lyre is the body of the Sun. The four strings are the four movements of the Sun: yearly, monthly, daily, oblique. The four tones – the Neate, the Hypate, and the twin Dorians – are the four threefold groupings of the signs, from which the four qualities of the seasons arise.

Calliope inspired Orpheus; Urania, Musaeus; Clio, Homer; Polyhymnia, Pindar; Erato, Sappho; Melpomene, Thamyras; Terpsichore, Hesiod; Thalia, Virgil; Euterpe, Ovid.

That same Phoebus who seized Linus is he who even now is arousing you, excellent Lorenzo: Phoebus, I say, who gave prophecy to your grandfather, Cosimo; the bow and the powers of healing to your father, Piero; and lastly, the lyre and songs to you.

Summary of Plato's *Statesman*

WHEN GOD and nature bring forth man through their action, they undoubtedly bring him forth in order to act: I mean, to act by the grace of divine influences. But just as there is one purpose for which nature creates a thumb, a second purpose for which she creates a hand or a foot, and a third purpose for which she creates the whole man, so there is one purpose to which she directs the individual man, a second purpose for the family, and a third for the state and the kingdom. Finally, there is what must be considered to be the best purpose: that for which God has created the whole of humanity.

No one should think, however, that although there is a fixed purpose for his own particular group, there is no purpose for the whole; or that, although order is inherent in all the parts of human life, there is confusion in the universal phenomenon of life; or lastly that, although the parts are mutually linked for the fulfilment of a single purpose, the whole itself is scattered abroad.

And so there is necessarily a definite purpose for humanity: this purpose is founded on activity centred on all that is close to perfection. By means of such activity humanity does its best to imitate all that is higher and to carefully regulate all that is lower; through knowledge it investigates natural phenomena; through prudence it takes care of human affairs; and through devotion it worships and honours things divine.

Such a purpose thus requires a dual life based equally on action and on contemplation, but in such a way that action is initiated for the sake of contemplation, which is more divine. What is more, the absolute perfection of this dual life needs so many, such great, and such varied adjuncts that it can be fulfilled not by a few men, or even by many, but only by the whole of humanity together.

However, it is impossible for such diverse peoples to be led by such diverse means to their single common purpose, unless it be by the One which draws all alike to itself through a single law. In the same way, craftsmen and servants who are widely disparate in nature and disposition, bringing a huge range of materials to the single form of a building, will never meet harmoniously in unity and will never build in the right manner, unless they are controlled by the single law of a single master builder.

This is why Plato was right when, in seeking a king to rule the world, he first brought forward a master builder and divided knowledge into three types. Central to the first type is cognition; to the second, action; to the third, doing. In the first type of knowledge he placed the Arithmetician and the Geometer; in the second type, the master builder; in the third, the craftsman and the servant.

In this way he showed that the function of the master builder is to be found midway between pure theory and pure service, although it has more of theory than of service. He also showed that the master builder not only judges in the manner of the Geometer but also commands the workers and always stands by the craftsman. Plato wishes the king to be exactly like this, both discerning the truth in the manner of the contemplatives and commanding that his own laws, and not those of others, be executed.

Then Plato, making use of a very fine distinction, which is quite essential for his definition and for knowledge, names the king, in Homeric fashion, 'the shepherd and protector of the human race'. That the king is the one shepherd of the whole human race, as if it were a flock, Plato shows by saying that God was once the shepherd of the human race and that under God there occurred the celebrated golden age of Saturn.

Plato deems that the king should also be called the helmsman of human life, as though it were a ship. He thus shows that the power exerted by all must be gathered to a single point, for human governance is identical to divine governance, and the one God is ruler of the whole world.

This is succinctly supported by the following arguments. Firstly, if you were to apportion three parts of the world – Asia, Africa, and Europe – to three kings, it would very likely happen that one day one of the kings would wage war on the other two, or that two of the kings would make war on the other, or at least that they would be compelled to quibble about boundaries or some other matter. And so among themselves they would have to ask for a verdict on the case from one of the three, or a fourth party would need to be made the referee.

But however it is done, there will have to be a judge, provided that the kings are willing to accept that his verdict will govern those between whom he is making his judgement; for if this is not the case the verdict will have no weight, and he will make his judgement in vain if it appears that it can be annulled by the kings or by wise men or others of similar power.

Thus a single king is required as judge of all the others: one who has the undoubted respect of all the others. Such a king, moreover, must be a model of virtue to his subjects. Most importantly, he will be above all the others, the one to whom every eye will turn. Even if he possessed the whole world, he would not desire another's kingdom or be envious of others. For these two, greed and envy, are the usual and the strongest causes of rapine and war.

And since every man cherishes most lovingly those things which are his own, he will most lovingly cherish all those people as his own, and he will likewise cherish and care for all nations. He will desire peace above all; he will prize calmness and an abundance of all good things, as a reflection of the empire which manifested under the rule of Octavian.

His subjects will live in the fullness of justice, since under this monarch there will be no possibility of escape for the unjust; and although his subjects will have least licence for wrong-doing, they will live in the greatest freedom, not being subject to tyrants or to a few men in power or to the rages of an insane populace, but being guided to the Good of all by a wise, just, and dutiful king, just as sailors are guided to harbour by the care of a true helmsman.

In this state of affairs, those who are ruled will care for their own interests through submission to the king, and the king will live not so much for himself as for all those who have been entrusted to his care by God. For, as is reasoned in the books of the *Republic*, right government establishes a governor for the sake of those governed: it does not establish the governed for the sake of the governor.

Again, Plato compares the king to a doctor, advising the king to impose a regimen, as if he were a doctor, and to apply restorative remedies in season and, if need be, out of season, upon the willing and occasionally upon the unwilling. But such a governor and preserver Plato calls 'citizen' more often than 'king', showing that such a person must, if possible, be considerate and gentle, so that he appears among citizens as a fellow-citizen, having a greater measure of foresight and justice and care rather than an excess of anything else.

Plato considers that any man who is clearly pre-eminent in foresight and justice has been chosen by God as the indisputable ruler of all, even if he has lived as a private citizen. But if there are several men among whom the differences are very slight with respect to these qualities, to such men, when brought together in a more or less harmonious body, royal power may be granted; but it must never be granted to a large group of men, for nowhere can there be found a large group of men worthy of such high power.

But one may infer from Plato's other books that his intention is for the power of government to be conveyed to the elders and the most upright of men, who then form a senate to be a partner for the king, like a republic of aristocrats. But the king, in association with the senate, would promulgate the laws, which no private citizen would be allowed to transgress and which could not be altered by the masses, although king and senate together would have the right, in accordance with the changes wrought by time, to adapt them, with care and equity, to circumstance and time and, if necessary, to change them.

In his letters Plato deems the king to be considered holy and to be established, in the manner of the Egyptians, as a priest, a high priest of the sacred mysteries. And since the king is holy, Plato, to prevent him from being defiled, does not allow him to play a part in judgements relating to execution, exile, or imprisonment. In this book likewise, as we have said, he demonstrates that such a monarchy is the best of all governments, while the worst is tyranny, which rules neither by law nor by lawful intent, but by whim and lust.

In the second place, he praises aristocrats and at the same time denounces the power of oligarchs. Thirdly, he praises government by the many, that is, democracy, provided that it is government according to law; but he denounces it if it is contrary to law.

After this he investigates the nature of kingly duty, that is, the duty to provide all that is needed for the human race and especially what is required for people to live good and happy lives. The king should wisely judge how many skills, and what kind of skills, are conducive to this end in times of peace and in times of war, whether by speaking or by acting both publicly and privately; and together with the senate he should exercise supreme rule over all citizens.

His principal duty, however, is to bring into harmony the hearts and minds of all the people, through the most judicious blending of courage with temperance; and in this he would be following the musicians, who measure out the sweetest harmonies by rightly commingling the high notes with the low notes.

For Plato shows – and shows in god-like fashion – that it is dangerous for souls to over-tension the string of courage and make the note too high, or to under-tension the string of temperance and make the note too low. If the first were to happen, men's souls would eventually become too savage; and if the second, they would become too effeminate. In the first case, they would, like enemies, attack their fellow-citizens and their country alike; and in the second case, they would safeguard neither themselves nor their country against enemies.

And so, what Plato thinks best is to produce a universal harmony of people's differing natures through the melodious blending of both these virtues.

But enough has now been said on the arrangement of the book.

In our *Theology* we have given an adequate exposition of what Plato says on the movement of the spheres, on providence, and on fate. In these discussions he undoubtedly teaches us, in an allegory, that we do not have a true and lawful king, unless it be He whom the King of heaven Himself has placed as a shepherd over us in heaven and on earth, a shepherd who fully represents the King of heaven Himself, not in name alone, but also in pattern of life.

Plato refers to two reigns, that of Jupiter and that of Saturn, and he attributes more happiness and prosperity to the reign of Saturn than to the reign of Jupiter. For the characteristics of Jupiter's reign are human activity and human life, while the mark of Saturn's reign is contemplation of the divine. As Plato teaches in *Cratylus*, Saturn, which is Cronos in Greek, includes purity and unassailable integrity of character. However, since he says that men live in bliss during the reign of Saturn, he is pointing out that, as long as some divine power holds sway in men's hearts, whereby actions conducive to contemplation are ordained, the human race will be blessed.

For my part, I shall quickly conclude his reasoning, the sooner to introduce a short allegory of this mystery. For he says that the current circuit of the world from east to west is Jovian and is decreed by fate, but that at some point in time there will be another circuit, opposed to this one, under Saturn and going in its turn from west to east. In this movement men will be born of their own free will and will move from maturity to youth; and foods will be liberally supplied to them according to their desire and without being requested, in a time of everlasting spring.

Plato calls Jupiter, as I think, the soul of the world, through whose law of destiny this manifest order of the manifest world is disposed. He has it, moreover, that the Jovian life of souls within elemental bodies is devoted to the senses and to action; whereas Saturn is the intellect which is supreme in the midst of the angels and by whose rays souls are illuminated and set ablaze beyond the angels, being continuously raised aloft with full power towards the intellectual life.

Whenever souls are turned to such a life, they are said to live under the reign of Saturn, insofar as they live by intelligence. Then they are said to be spontaneously re-born in such a life because, of their own choice, they are shaped anew for the better.

Again, they grow younger every day; that is, as the days are measured there, they evermore continue to flourish. Paul the Apostle says: 'The inward man is renewed day by day.'

Finally, they are freely and abundantly supplied with foods in a time of everlasting spring because it is not through the senses or through the discipline of necessity, but through the light at the heart of their being and with utter tranquillity and enjoyment of life, that they delight in the wonderful reflections of Truth itself.

Summary of *Protagoras*

T HERE SURVIVES among the Greeks that absolutely true saying about Plato to the effect that Phoebus begat two sons in particular, Aesculapius and Plato: Aesculapius to heal bodies, and Plato to heal souls. All the followers of Socrates bear witness that Socrates, too, had been sent by God to purify men's souls.

Now disease of the soul is seen to consist in false opinions and bad ways of living. But there is no easier way of imparting such a great evil to innocent souls than by means of the Sophists.

Philosophers, of course, are those who assiduously seek the truth from simple love of truth itself, while Sophists pursue opinion from love of opinion. For Sophists are like traders and dealers in learning: they indiscriminately assemble from all directions a variety of opinions which they can think about or talk about in any way they choose and which they later sell like merchandise to rich young men in exchange for wealth and vainglory. Thus they possess nothing of any worth, whether they are learning and teaching what is true and good or whether they are learning and teaching the opposite; but they create confusion and pour out streams of errors in all directions every day, without any principle of true discrimination, solely to amass riches and to chase after fame at its lowest level.

To this end, youths and grown men who value the Sophists so highly for their opinion of wisdom and their false show of eloquence are obliged each day to quaff the venomous draughts of these men's false opinions and vile ways; for evil ways come in the wake of false opinions and are easily transmitted to their followers by grasping and ambitious teachers, who are nonetheless held in high regard.

Plato, therefore, taking compassion upon souls that expose themselves to dangers so readily and with such commitment, exerts all his powers over and over again, in the person of Socrates, to denounce the wicked, venemous Sophists, so that men who wish to learn may take care to keep well away from the beguiling songs of the Sirens and the deadly draughts of Circe.

Yet he does not blast them with open invective, lest he himself should appear caught up in agitation or in hatred against them, and lest they and their followers should retaliate with the poisoned barbs of a tongue that knows no shame. Therefore it is partly through irony and partly through laughter, often through jest and play, and more often through an honourable defence, that he seeks to remove unmerited authority from the Sophists.

In the *Sophist* he perfects his aim with keen penetration; in *Gorgias*, with the height of refinement; in *Hippias*, with great urbanity; in *Euthydemus*, with subtlety; in *Protagoras*, with skill; and such is his common practice. But on all occasions he presents Sophists who make a show of everything as boastful and ostentatious, as well as audacious and avaricious.

At the beginning of the debate he presents them as fairly competent, but as gradually becoming less and less competent, until in the end they are shown as completely incompetent, with no understanding of the nature or extent of the weightier aspects under consideration; and when they make universal protestations, he proves that they know nothing at all.

So far it is enough to have referred initially to the Sophists in our writings on all the dialogues of Plato in which they are mentioned. Let us now proceed to *Protagoras*.

From the prophetess Diotima Socrates has learnt the art of love, by which he has come to know that from the impressions made by physical beauty we can use our judgement to hunt out the beauty of the soul, the beauty of the angelic mind, and the beauty of God. Socrates teaches this art of love wherever he is. Plato expounds this art on many occasions, but particularly in the *Symposium* and the *Phaedrus*.

He presents the same art at the beginning of this book. For this reason he adds that he loves men no less than youths, and shortly afterwards he declares that he also loves older men, provided that they appear wiser. Later, while using all his skill to warn Hippocrates, a young man who is very eager to undergo discipline, not to commit himself blindly to any particular discipline, Socrates is giving us, too, a strong reminder to put care for the soul far above care for the body, and to be very careful not to absorb harmful disciplines, for these inflict more harm on our soul than poison does on our body.

He quickly proceeds to put before our eyes, in the manner of an artist, the arrogance and vanity of the Sophists. He also shows the extent to which credulous young people admire the Sophists' ostentation and are captivated by their pandering ways.

Then he arrives at those principles which are of the greatest importance in life and in which the Sophists take so much pride: he enquires after every kind of virtue, especially that civic virtue by which affairs private, domestic, and public are disposed in accordance with the highest Good through the true principle which Plato, in almost all his dialogues, seeks as the one that is more needful than all the others.

At the same time he shows that this is not in any way to be sought by the Sophists, but may to some extent be sought by philosophers, who understand the True and who honour the Good and thus are certainly able, with God as their guide, to proceed directly to this way of life.

But let us now return to the Sophist, who cannot be given such a virtue through example or taught it through discussion, as may be clearly seen from the fact that he himself is unacquainted with virtue and does not observe the proper order of discussion. For when he is here asked by Socrates whether or not virtue can be taught, Protagoras, like one ignorant of the true art of debate, immediately takes it upon himself to show that virtue can be taught, even before the question has been broached as to what virtue is or into how many parts it may be divided.

Socrates, however, wishing to test the Sophist, reasons that virtue cannot be taught. His words are more or less as follows: When a craftsman whose art can be taught by qualified instructors is publicly asked for advice, no one is vouchsafed this advice except those who have learnt an art of this kind from the instructors themselves and have also practised it themselves. But when there is a discussion about public matters, which relate to civic virtue, almost everyone is admitted indiscriminately, and no one is asked whether and when and from whom he received civic knowledge, as if everyone understands that it cannot be learnt in the established schools.

Moreover, if civic virtue were handed down from one person to another, men greatly renowned for it would bequeath something as precious as this to their descendants by some kind of hereditary law.

In response to these arguments, Protagoras shows in a long roundabout way that virtue can be taught. In his words Protagoras puts forward some mysteries of the ancients as being worthy of note. For although he is a Sophist, it is to his credit that he has actually read some good works; and although in Plato's account he speaks at great length, it is to his credit that he introduces some useful points.

The theologians of ancient times relate that living beings once lay hidden under the earth: that is to say, the seeds of things were pre-existent in the primordial substance of the world. In particular, they say that Jupiter, the god who creates the world, compounded living beings from the elements by means of the lesser gods, the stars. They say that the gods, through the agency of the daemons, furnished the living beings with the means and supports needful for life, so that Prometheus, who represents the highest level of daemons, might equip men.

But Epimetheus, who represents the host of the lower daemons, upheld the irrational; and this is quite lawful, for the higher daemons support incorporeal and rational nature, while the lower daemons support corporeal and irrational nature. But the more Epimetheus and the lower nature support the irrational in matters pertaining to the body, the more Prometheus and the higher providence seem to give counsel to men in matters pertaining to the soul. For when he bestowed the principle of art, he revealed the skilful maker of all that nature has granted to the beasts.

However, he received this art, together with fire, through the offices of Minerva and Vulcan. Within the art Minerva keeps her skill, Vulcan his power, and fire its materials. Now these twin divinities, Minerva and Vulcan, are considered to be firstly within the actual Ideas of the arts, secondly within the powers of Mercury and Mars, and finally within the daemons which govern the arts.

Prometheus, therefore, ruler of the rational soul, transferred the activity of art from all of these to man. But because that divine gift was present, man, through his kinship with the divine, worshipped God before he could speak and before he could practise any of the arts; for through its wonderful power the divine gift raises him to the divine before sending him forth to human activities.

The fact that Prometheus was afflicted with pain on account of that gift shows that the daemon which takes care of us and in which emotions are possible is moved by compassion towards us, thinking that through the very gift of reason which it has given, or rather awakened, we lead a life on earth that is more wretched than that of the beasts, since it is more disturbed and more tearful.

Taking note of this, Pythagoras put Epimetheus before Prometheus in this respect, which is rather like saying 'it repenteth me that I have made' man. In the same way, remember that, according to Moses, man was created from earth and was created last. Again, in the Mosaic tradition, the world had a beginning.

But these matters are dealt with elsewhere. It is said in *Philebus* that it was through the agency of Prometheus that the art of dialectic, together with fire, was given to us by the gods. For when the art of dialectic divides universals into particulars, it shows the movement of things from the higher realms; on the other hand, when it correctly resolves particulars into universals, it shows the return of things to the higher realms; when it defines and demonstrates, it shows the existence of things as being independent in the higher realms, but dependent here.

That is why the faculty of dialectic is a divine gift, for it portrays the divine order of the universe. It is said to have been given with fire because fire, like dialectic, divides, resolves, defines, and demonstrates; and because the rational faculty, like fire, illumines the intellect, fires the will, and raises both on high.

But when it is said that Prometheus was unable to bestow civic virtue, which is absolutely necessary for men's safety, because such a virtue resides in the abode of Jupiter, to which Prometheus is not allowed to rise, what is to be understood is that the function of civic virtue is not only to govern human affairs but also to govern the arts and to put individual things into order with other individual things, and finally to direct all things towards the common form of all. But this is the very function of Jupiter himself in the universe, and it manifests in the human race as the function of civic knowledge.

Thus it is quite right that the bestowal of this power upon us from on high should be related to Jupiter himself. For universal power belongs to the universal providence of Jupiter. But the providence of the daemons is particular and constrained; and this is why it cannot ascend to the citadel of Jupiter, for providence which is more confined and at a lower level lacks the strength to become equal to that which is unrestricted and at the highest level.

Thus Jupiter, through the agency of Mercury, the messenger who interprets the divine will, writes on our hearts the laws of civic knowledge, that is to say, the decrees of his will that relate to the welfare of society and of mankind. He writes them, I say, at the beginning, as the *Timaeus* openly teaches, and he also writes them every day through the agency of the angels, who interpret the divine will to us.

Thus, deep within us, presides the judge, the inextinguishable light of reason, the just discrimination between true and false, between good and evil, and the inexorable goad of conscience. Through this law, which has been imparted to all, God directs all things to the common good so fully that He raises all flames aloft through their lightness. From this innate law the written law then takes its rise. This is what Plato discloses at the very beginning of his book of *Laws* when he says that laws had their beginning not in man but in God Himself.

But to return to the dialogue in hand: Plato adds that Jupiter established through Mercury the law by which all are happy to partake of civic life, especially since this law alone is the bond of the state. He says that civic life itself, maintained by justice and modesty, has been sent down to us all from heaven so that anyone who is later found without the least trace of this virtue will be put to death as a bane on the state.

But he first named modesty, and then temperance, for innate modesty is the basis of temperance. Temperance in citizens moderates the feelings of each citizen and shapes his actions, while justice directs each citizen's actions to be of benefit to others.

We should remember, however, that civic life is circumscribed in a private person by precisely these two things, whereas, according to Plato, prudence should be added to these two in the public citizen. This would be quite sufficient in a time of peace, but in a time of war the addition of courage is necessary; and that is the full description of civic life.

Now, after this, Protagoras, drawing on the common view held by men, confirms that all are necessarily partakers of this virtue, especially because a man who openly declares his injustice is generally considered insane, which indicates that everyone believes public justice to be so vital to the state that even a person who lacks it should at least put on a show of possessing it.

But when Protagoras has later shown that civic virtue is the most important of all the virtues for all people and that a disposition towards it has been divinely imparted to us as if it were some tinder or a seed, he then proceeds to prove that civic virtue and other virtues – for they are all included within it – could not be allocated by nature or by chance as an absolute and steadfast disposition, but such a disposition has been acquired purely by teaching and by custom.

The first reason he gives to support his proof is the one which demonstrates that men are at no time in the habit of basing their approval or disapproval of anyone on what happens either through nature or by chance, but that they always praise the actions of virtue and condemn the actions of vice. Then he sets out the training for childhood and adolescence in a long series of stages: under parents, nurses, and tutors, grammarians, musicians, and gymnasts, and under the laws.

In this way he shows that the whole organisation of life is a strenuous attempt to give less scope to vices and more scope to virtues, with the implication that vices and virtues do not arise from fortune or fate but from choice and practice. In the meantime he refers to the view of the ancients – that vices should be punished – as being worthy of consideration: that a man should never be punished for doing wrong, but should be punished lest he do further wrong or lest another do wrong by following his example. He also answers the objections raised by Socrates.

From all the subsequent discussions, however, we shall hold to that golden opinion of the ancients which lies deep in our heart: firstly, that God Himself provides and cares for our life and safety in all places and in all ways; secondly, that civic virtue is a divine gift (in case anyone considers that he can govern the state properly and prosperously without divine grace), for Plato confirms this in the *Laws* and elsewhere when he says, 'Just as a multitude of animals cannot be led by another animal except under the guidance of a human shepherd, so a multitude of men cannot be happily ruled by one king unless that one king is himself ruled by God.' And in the same way he shows in *Theages* and *Meno* that the ability to rule is received from God alone.

But Protagoras the Sophist has seen what he himself wishes.

Finally, we shall remember what a great need there is for the inviolable justice that has been sent from heaven, provided that our ears are in total resonance with the words of the ancients who said, 'Before civic virtue was sent from heaven, wretched human beings were unable to live in isolation for fear of being rent by wild beasts wherever they were; and they were unable, on the other hand, to live in communities for fear of being torn to pieces by each other.' And so justice alone eventually granted us the safety which all the arts together were unable to grant.

After this, not wishing the Sophist to be admired by his hearers for repeating some good things which he has received from others, Socrates uses a method of refutation that is ironic, urbane, and ingenious, to make him an object of mockery in the eyes of those present. For, after speaking so splendidly about virtue, he asks whether virtue is single or multiple; and if it is multiple, whether or not the parts

71

constitute the whole; again, whether the parts are similar or dissimilar to each other and to the whole.

To this Protagoras does not know how to respond aright; how to define or distinguish the virtues; how to say on what basis they are similar or dissimilar; or – and this is most disgraceful in a debate – how to avoid being easily led into a situation where he frequently contradicts himself. But when through his ignorance of how to respond, Protagoras begins to decline an answer, and Socrates gives the impression that he is going to leave, the Sophist is recalled to the debate by those listening.

The first thing to show itself in this interchange is the superstitious curiosity of Prodicus the Sophist regarding words; and then comes the somewhat puffed-up pride in public oratory exhibited by Hippias the Sophist. Finally, Protagoras, having been recalled to the debate, makes a very inappropriate and clumsy digression into the realm of song and poetry, asking Socrates about the meaning of some passage composed by the poet Simonides: a passage which Socrates, expounding the intention of Simonides, quickly proves was not understood by the poet himself, who, as it were, said that it was difficult to become a good man, and impossible to remain a good man.

This is where you will hear that the wisdom of the ancients was expressed in the fewest possible words; that much can be embraced in brief compass; that there is a need for a man whose learning knows no bounds; that no one commits evil or base actions of his own will, but commits them through ignorance; and finally, when the discussion follows the principles of dialectic, that poetry is to be set aside. At this point the Sophist again declines to give an answer, and only with some difficulty is he called back again by those present.

Then Socrates reverts to the earlier discussion about virtue, asking whether there are many parts composing a single virtue and on what basis they are related one to another. But Protagoras slips up once more, affirming that there are other virtues which are very similar one to another, which he had not admitted earlier, setting courage far apart from all the others, and agreeing that men can be courageous without prudence and the remaining virtues. In this position he is then obliged to contradict himself and to admit that neither courage nor any other virtue can stand without prudence.

There follow many points of discussion about good and evil, for prudence is the knowledge of how to choose good and avoid evil. Yet there is a doubt as to whether good and evil are fundamentally the same as pleasure and pain; and there is neither a full affirmation of this identity nor an obviously complete denial. But there is more on this question in *Gorgias, Philebus,* and other works.

However, it is proved exhaustively that prudence itself – in which are found both the aim of life, which is knowledge, and the choice of pathways leading to this aim – is the head and leader of the moral virtues; and this is affirmed so strongly that virtues are seen as forms of knowledge or prudence, while vices are seen as forms of ignorance or imprudence. It is stated later that all sins proceed from ignorance, and that no man would ever choose evil unless he were beguiled by some image of the good, and he would never shun the good unless he were terrified by some image of evil.

But if anyone says that a man who can distinguish good from evil will turn from the good and towards evil because he is overpowered by pleasure or by some other delight of the senses, Socrates denies this, asserting that the very thing that is said to be overpowered by delight is nothing other than ignorance, but that knowledge of all that is within us and around us is infinitely powerful and can never be overpowered by anything. He concludes that knowledge is conducive primarily, or rather absolutely, to virtue and bliss, whereas ignorance leads equally to their opposites.

And he lays a heavy hand on Protagoras once more for contradicting himself and for using the preposterous method of beginning to differentiate virtue before defining it, and likewise of discussing whether it can be taught. Socrates even pretends that he, too, has been led into a state of self-contradiction, insofar as he has followed an erring Sophist, and he advises us to imitate, all through our lives and with all the strength we can muster, the providence of Prometheus rather than the haste of Epimetheus.

Summary of *Euthydemus*

I N *EUTHYDEMUS*, as in many of his other writings, Plato – a man noted for his love towards others – seeks to turn minds born for the contemplation of serious matters away from the fripperies of the Sophists, showing that when there is a discussion of the deepest import the Sophists play games and always disappoint the hopes of their listeners.

He describes the Sophists in different ways on different occasions, and here he describes them as prying, ostentatious disputants in an altercation of words, quick to refute whatever is said, whether true or false.

He shows first the grasping nature of the Sophists, for Euthydemus and Dionysidorus, brother Sophists, are prepared to teach for a fee the military art, in which they glory and which no one has ever sold before. Plato then shows the extent of their ambition, for they make a show of their judicial knowledge together with their military knowledge, and of both these alongside their sophistry, although these three subjects are, in fact, widely disparate.

Thirdly, Plato shows what empty shells they are, as they move in their old age from facts to words, and from the study of truth to the telling of lies. He shows in the fourth place how despicable they are; for in a short time, two years at most, anyone can acquire this art of scoffing. He shows, fifthly, how dangerous they are; for who would be surprised that simple youths are easily ensnared by the tinsel craftiness of the Sophists and then imbued with false opinions and pernicious habits, when even Socrates himself, an old man full of wisdom, pretends to be caught by the same bait and to be hastening in wonder towards the schools of the Sophists?

Moreover, even that spirit of Socrates, which seems incapable of being deceived by anyone, gives the impression of being deceived by the sophistical tricks of these scoundrels. At the same time, even in his old age, Socrates advises us, in his frequent allusions to schools for boys, schools of music, and the principles of language, not to neglect so much as the smallest detail in the perfection of discipline; not to shut ourselves off, as we often do, from zealous application to discipline; but to follow Solon in thinking that we should continue to learn as long as our life endures.

Accordingly, because the Sophists are never aware of irony at their expense – indeed, there is nothing in praise of them, however high-sounding it may be, that they do not believe with the greatest readiness and receive with open arms – he now makes clear to us two things in particular: the first is that it is impossible to find anything more hollow than these scoundrels; the second, that people who eagerly set out to deceive others have no difficulty at all in falling prey to their own deceptions.

Moreover, the fact that such impostors never bestow the virtue which they promise and never encourage anyone to practise it, but always resort to the usual empty talk about words and have no hesitation in treating such talk as serious in preference to other studies, which they regard as games, shows us three things in particular. The first is that men who are not themselves graced with virtue can never teach it, either in theory or by example. The second is that men who are too caught up in words never pursue good things and never transmit good things to others. The third is that men who promise a great many things with the utmost readiness keep their promises least of all.

Furthermore, in order to teach virtue to the Sophists, Socrates draws to himself a horde of very many rich disciples, extremely ambitious and grasping. But here, through the person of Crito, we are warned not to entrust the care of our soul to anyone without proper consideration. Yet the fact that Socrates entreats the Sophists as if they were gods when they are promising to give virtue shows clearly that virtue is to be sought from God Himself, and that men endowed with virtue should be considered divine. Again, his view that men through their zeal for virtue are blest above kings shows clearly that a man endowed with virtue is king of himself first and is then king of kings.

Furthermore, in his care for Cleinias, Socrates demonstrates how much attentiveness and love we need to show when looking after the youth. But soon, through the promises made by the haughtiest of the Sophists, the mountains give birth and a ridiculous mouse will be born. Yet we should note here the hyperbolical irony used by Socrates to deride men of no substance; then the unparalleled futility of the scoundrels who consistently proffer words – and the most inapposite words at that – instead of deeds and who, having promised encouragement in the search for wisdom, fall back upon puerile stupidities.

Then Socrates says that the entire school of Sophists is but a game of words, and that they utterly conceal the nature of things, and that their crafty barbs can be neutralised only by an exposition of words and by distinctions of meaning.

Then, with the rarest irony, he beseeches the Sophists to come to serious matters after their games; and he puts forward a method, in accordance with which he earnestly desires from them some encouragement to follow philosophy. Through such a method he first describes happiness as generally understood: living well. Then he shows that living well consists either in pursuing things at will or in making proper use of them. And he concludes with inferences from both sides: wisdom, only when followed at will and used aright, alone makes men happy. And at that point there is such order in his method of induction that, provided wisdom is pursued at will through all parts of life and also used aright, the attendant aim in the whole of life, and also the supreme Good, is conveyed by this same wisdom, which consists in being pursued at will and being used aright.

But in the course of the reasoning the brilliant thinking illuminates the base tenet of the Stoic school that external, physical things should be called neutral and common rather than good or evil, whereas wisdom should truly be called good, and foolishness should be called evil; for through wisdom all good things reach us, while through foolishness all evils come our way; and thus wisdom alone can make us happy.

But because the power that leads to happiness consists wholly in knowledge, three names for happiness are said to have been established by the early Greek writers: Eudaemonia, Eutychia, and Eupragia. The first means awareness of the good; the second, pursuit of the good; while the third means the use of the good. Wisdom brings them all to perfection for us.

Here and elsewhere Plato says that in some way this knowledge of the good is the whole of virtue; that wisdom is the knowledge of the absolute divine Good; that prudence is the knowledge of good and evil things pertaining to man; that justice is the knowledge of how to apportion good and evil things according to men's merits; that courage is the knowledge of daring and fearing with respect to good and evil things; and finally, that temperance is the knowledge of accepting and shunning with respect to good and evil things.

Here we need to remember first and foremost that in this dialogue and in many others Plato is giving the meaning of wisdom not as it is acquired by human effort, but rather as it is customarily imparted to purified minds by divine providence; for the soul that is united to this body is thereby rendered incapable of handling matters that are far removed from the body and is blinded like an owl by the extreme brightness of things divine. This is why the Socratic exhortation to wisdom is not in the realm of speculation but concerns how we live. Being eventually purified in this way, the soul obtains from God wisdom and knowledge and prudence.

With these words Socrates, while pretending to entreat from the Sophists an exhortation to practise philosophy, which is the zeal for wisdom, is at the same time, through this very apposite irony, giving them wonderful words of encouragement to practise philosophy themselves. The Sophists, however, do not yet take hold of such encouragement either for themselves or even for others, but keep churning out their usual follies, which shows how tenaciously human nature, if born in adverse circumstances or if badly brought up, clings to defects and foolishness.

At this point we should take very careful note of Plato's divine view, by which we are directed, in the pursuit of wisdom, not only to endure with patience any misfortune, loss, toil, or servitude, but also, if we hope to eventually become better as a result of our own destruction, to surrender ourselves to the one who has foretold this, to be flayed, dissolved, and utterly destroyed, which shows the extent to which the good of the soul surpasses things corporeal and how much esteem is due to those most courageous Christian martyrs of old. And this is reflected in the words, 'He that loveth his soul in this world shall lose it, but he that will lose it here shall receive it again in life eternal.'

Hence Socrates, refuting the fallacies of the Sophists, shows how easily sophisms can be turned against the Sophists, especially when he obliges them to contradict themselves and to admit complete absurdities. Then, adopting a method similar to the previous one, he proves that those listening receive nothing from the Sophists, and that the Sophists themselves, as if they were very rich men, cannot be recalled to virtue.

But since in the course of the discussion he often repeats these three names – wisdom, knowledge, and prudence – we should take note that when he speaks with great care he defines wisdom as knowledge of the divine, knowledge as knowledge of things natural, and prudence as knowledge of things human; but when he speaks with less care he uses the word 'knowledge' in all of these three senses; and when he speaks without restriction he uses any one of these words to stand for all three.

Furthermore, he refers to two kinds of arts: those arts which produce works, and those arts which make use of the works produced. And since the art which uses the work of the other art prescribes for it the purpose of making the work and provides a model for completing the work, we are justified in ascribing greater worth to the 'using' art than to the 'making' art. Note here that Plato belittles the making art and magnifies the using art so much that he very clearly wishes anyone who can at will turn all substances into gold or even acquire immortality for men to receive no personal advantage from such a vast mass of gold or from immortality unless he knows how to make use of it.

Again, note that the common abuse of the art of rhetoric, such as is practised by the Sophists, is directly repudiated as a kind of wicked enchantment which always strives to infect men's minds with poisonous disturbances. For a similar reason he denounces the abuse of poetry in other dialogues. But because in this dialogue he names dialectic among the arts to be enumerated – let me not say, as some do, 'dialecticen', since 'dialectica' sounds more Latin to me – one needs to remember that Plato takes logic to mean the art that organises the rules of names, of speeches, and of debates, while he takes dialectic to mean the penetrating investigation made by a man in pursuit of philosophy, making use of these rules to study the causes of things and especially of things divine, from which the highest causes of subsequent things, too, are received; and this is why dialectic means to Plato mainly what theology means to us.

In the same place he calls the royal and civic art, which is prudence, the art of governing the human race in happiness and prosperity. Whether this art be for the individual or for the community, in one place or in many, he calls it equally both civic and royal. To it, as to a queen, he subjects all of the faculties of acting and doing by which it ordains laws and which it employs as its instruments and servants. He likewise subjects to theology all the types of knowledge that are used in reflection: they are to theology as the private arts are to the royal art.

For this reason, while Socrates is searching, within a method that is in turn linked to a higher method, for the power most conducive to happiness, he rightly sets others aside and resorts to the royal art and to theology, especially since happiness consists in the best use of things, and the royal art and theology strive through all possible means to convey to everyone the best use of reflecting, acting, and doing.

This is Plato's message in the *Philebus*, in the last book of the *Laws*, and also in the books of the *Republic*, where he instructs the man who will guide the human race to happiness, first in theology and then in civic studies, asserting that the divine Idea of the Good is perceived at length and with difficulty by the true theologian alone, and that, unless it is perceived, nothing can be rightly done or prosperously ordered, in private or in public.

Although this is the situation, Socrates does not think it right for these mysteries to be revealed here in the presence of youths and Sophists. For the way adopted by Socrates is to exhort the youth only, to refute the Sophists only, and finally to teach genuine seekers. Here, therefore, under cover of irony and pretence such as we have described, he alludes to the mysteries and he feigns doubt and pretends to suffer giddiness as if in the midst of giddy Sophists. But perhaps he is feigning doubt on the question of whether theology and civic virtue are more important than happiness, because he frequently confirms that the perfection of theology and the perfection of civic duty can be obtained by no human means, but only by divine inspiration.

And so he is right not to put his trust in human powers but to refer happiness to divine grace, to which he has undoubtedly referred both the wisdom of theology and the prudence of civic discipline. In short, it is in this way that we should accept all these things, so that even our human duties may prepare our minds for happiness, especially those duties which are most properly directed by theological and civic training. But the all-merciful goodness of God Himself finally bestows the supreme Good upon men who have turned to Him through these duties as if through intermediaries.

I had decided to bring this subject, or rather this commentary, to a valid conclusion at this point, but I am prevented by the need to examine the aim of Socrates' frequent use of irony, which always conceals his own good thoughts but often represents the thoughts of the Sophists as good; which always detracts from Socrates as much as it assigns to the arrogant on many occasions; and which, through jests and quips, frequently has the effect – quite often beyond all belief – of making his listeners more virtuous through his own self-deprecation; but which, by praising the haughty beyond the bounds of credibility, gives them an arrogance that is open to universal derision.

Indeed, those who receive excessive praise from Socrates, if they are not completely lost, correct themselves in a confusion of embarrassment; but if they are already completely lost, it is not they themselves but those present who, on the basis of that reproof, are very careful to avoid such a ridiculous empty show of arrogance. Yet there is something about Socrates' irony that is quite artistic, courteous, elegant, and charming. He finds greater security by being in accord with the truth and by turning aside from hatred. He skilfully disguises his own public declaration and openly disparages himself before being found to disparage someone else privately; and – of the greatest importance when correcting evil ways – he shuns all trace of abusiveness.

Towards the end of this dialogue it is in this way, of course, that he reflects upon the blame attaching to the jeering of the Sophists, and he considers three main points. The first is that the most upright of men disdain such trumpery. The second is that fallacies are self-contradictory. The third is that, within two days, even children understand that these are mere trifles.

Soon afterwards he moves down from the Sophist to the rhetorician, for they both make a false show of civic virtue, as we read in *Gorgias*; and the Sophist feigns the contemplative nature of the philosopher, while the rhetorician feigns the philosopher's moral training, both far from the truth. But Socrates shows that while rhetoricians and orators profess to be both philosophers and statesmen, they are completely useless in both capacities.

He finally concludes the dialogue with a pair of excellent sentiments. The first is that you should take more care that your children are *well* than that your children *are*; and that you leave them *good* rather than leaving them *goods*. The second is that you should practise philosophy fully, for philosophy is of God; and you should not set aside such a precious possession on account of any who falsely profess it or lyingly slander it.

Summary of the *Lesser Hippias*

MARVELLOUS IS the goodness of Socrates and our Plato, for in many ways and in all places it takes the greatest care to ensure that credulous youths are not caught in the treacherous snares of the Sophists or, if already caught, do not perish; and Plato is quite justified in employing two dialogues, the *Greater* and the *Lesser*, to assail Hippias of Elis, the most arrogant and the most deceitful of the Sophists.

In the *Greater* he shows that Hippias, who professes to speak of all that is most beautiful, has not the slightest knowledge of what beauty is. In the *Lesser* he shows that Hippias, who is boasting that he is better than all others at distinguishing a man who lies from a man who speaks truthfully, is completely wrong in his definition of both; and it thus becomes evident that Hippias, the most arrogant of all, is also the most ignorant of all and appears as the most incapable of all.

I merely allude to the fact that Plato depicts him, in his usual way with Sophists, as boastful and brash and grasping, offering words in all things but in fact proffering nothing, and boasting of all that is greatest while stumbling over the smallest.

But to return to the definition of a man who lies and a man who speaks truthfully: a man who lies should rightly have been described as lying as much as he wishes in whatever way he can and knows how to; while a man who speaks truthfully speaks what is true as much as he wishes and in whatever way he can and knows how to. But Hippias, a master unskilled in any of the arts and the most muddled discriminator between the man who speaks truthfully and the man who lies, defines them the other way round and says that the liar is the man who has full power and full knowledge of how to lie whenever he wishes, while the man who speaks truthfully is the one who has the power and knowledge to speak what is true whenever he wishes.

From this he is obliged to admit, firstly, that liars possess power, knowledge, prudence, and wisdom; and secondly, that good men are wise about those things in relation to which they have power. Thirdly, through inferences drawn from individual arts, he is compelled to confess that in any matter or art the same man is both truthful and a liar, which he had denied at the outset, for the man who has the most expertise in anything wields the most power in this sphere and knows both how to speak truthfully and how to lie, whichever he chooses. Fourthly, Hippias is led to concede that the truthful man is no whit better than the liar, for just as the truthful man is able and good at speaking the truth, so the liar seems able and good at telling lies.

Then Socrates leads the Sophist into a doubt as to whether or not the man who lies willingly commits a more grievous offence than the man who lies unwillingly. The Sophist does not know how to solve this problem, and Socrates refuses to solve it for him. But the solution is as follows: in matters pertaining to morals, they err more. The man, however, who lies unwillingly is in a different position.

Then there is a debate on whether people do greater wrong if they sin intentionally or through weakness or ignorance; and it is proved by a long, inductive digression that in matters pertaining to nature and art and their ancillaries the wrong committed through impotence or ignorance is more serious than the wrong perpetrated through ill-will, because the goodness of nature resides in power, while the goodness of art resides in both power and knowledge; and evil therefore resides in the opposites.

But from these points Socrates moves Hippias beyond the main subject to ways of living, drawing the same conclusion in the sphere of morals as in the sphere of nature and art. Although Socrates understands that this cannot be so, he is at pains to make it clear that the Sophist has no inkling of it. Indeed, in these matters pertaining to intention and ways of living, more harm is done through ill-will – the intention to sin – than through impotence or ignorance.

Finally, Socrates states that justice is either power or knowledge or both. He knew that the third possibility was will – for justice resides mainly in will – but he did not wish to add it, making it clear that he wanted to keep the Sophist in the dark.

But let us now conclude the subject with precepts established earlier: teach ungrudgingly; learn without embarrassment; always thank the teacher; do not claim for yourself the discoveries made by others.

Summary of *Charmides*, Concerning Temperance

S OCRATES' WORK in this dialogue is to encourage everyone to practise temperance, but he gives particular encouragement to three groups: those who are in their youth, those who are noble, and those who are beautiful.

He wishes to encourage the young because medicine needs to be administered quickly to diseases: miss the early stages and it is too late to prepare the medicine, now that the ailments have grown strong through long delay.

He also wishes to encourage those who are noble, because he wants to demonstrate that true nobility is to be found in virtue and, further, because the majority of noble people are an example to others and, being admitted every day to civil power, inflict very serious harm on the human race if they are evil.

Lastly, he wishes to encourage those who are beautiful, because they are depraved more readily than all others by the practices of the profligates and thus stand in greater need of medicine. The beautiful, moreover, must take pains to ensure that, just as nature has granted transient beauty to their bodies, so they themselves will in turn give back to God, the Lord of nature, the eternal beauty of their souls. But in spite of the fact that our outer appearance may please many with its beauty, we are not allowed to let what is within us be displeasing through its deformity.

Although all the parts of this dialogue – and especially the parts about love – present a marvellous allegory, as does the *Song of Solomon*, I have changed some elements and even left some out. For things which sounded harmonious to the delicate ears of the Greeks perhaps fall discordantly upon coarser ears. For the same reason, Aristarchus, a lover of Homer and, indeed, of Plato, said that anything discordant was not of Plato but of Cronos.

But in the first part three things in particular should be noted which transpose love from this bodily form to incorporeal beauty. The first is

Socrates' statement that he discerns no difference between this beautiful person and that beautiful person, for all beautiful people please him equally; this is like saying that one need not tarry within the form of a single body but should rise up to the beauty that is common to the whole type. Since this is one within many, it refers to the simple Idea of beauty above the many. And so, just as, in our consideration, we move from the individual to the type, and from the type to the Idea, so we are directed to proceed from love of this form to love of the common form and thence to love of the ideal form.

Socrates adds that bodily beauty is not to be loved for its own sake but is to be thought of as an image of divine beauty.

Finally, he directs us to lay bare the soul, after consigning the form of the body to a humbler place, to look upon the natural glory of the soul, and to use it carefully in its application to study. And in the meantime he apprehends Chaerephon and says something about stripping his body, as if in the wrestling-school. And it is quite right for his encouragement to practise temperance to begin with the beauty of the body. For this kind of temperance is of lines and colours; but from this he moves next to the health of the body, which is another kind of temperance, the temperance of the humours and the limbs.

He moves, thirdly, from this to the beauty of the soul itself, which is the temperance of emotion, the moderation of movements. In cognition, too, there is likewise a temperance, consisting of a harmonious correspondence between the faculty of intelligence and all that is perceived, so that Pythagoras was justified in saying that temperance is the most beneficial of all the virtues, the preserver of human society both for the community and for the individual, especially since justice, too, is a kind of temperance, that is, an appropriate moderation in the actions of exchange and distribution.

Indeed, although temperance is really about restraining violent passions and pleasures, it is also applied by analogy to cutting off all desires and to moderating every action, so that even the work of courage is executed under the moderating influence of audacity and fear; and in the same way the work of justice is moderated by rewards and punishments, and the office of liberality is moderated by entreaty; and in the end the welfare of the entire life is subjected to maximum moderation. Hence the maxim of Pythagoras: Measure is the best thing of all.

But remember that in the *Phaedo* those men are said to be intemperate who abstain from pleasures for the sake of physical pleasure. For he wishes human actions to be related to purification of the mind, in the pursuit of wisdom and of likeness to God. But such is the excellence of wisdom that it is observed by all skilful craftsmen in their work, and its power preserves not only every body beneath the moon but also the heavens themselves and the universe, as is confirmed in *Gorgias* by the testimony of the wise. This is reflected in the saying, 'God disposes all things sweetly.' Again, 'He disposes all things according to number, weight, and measure.' But let us now return to the dialogue.

When Socrates, in accordance with the view of the Magi, forbids the cure of the body before that of the soul, he is clearly reproving those who disregard things of the greatest import whilst caring for things of the least import, like men who seek out cures for their horses and dogs but never consult doctors about the ills of their own body and soul. They put their possessions into good order, down to the smallest detail, themselves remaining quite disordered in soul and body. With untempered soul they temper the lyre. Each day they handle outlandish things with great care, but neglect what is truly theirs.

Of course, everything apart from the soul is outlandish for us. This is why he calls medicine for the body a triviality, a fragile bagatelle subject to all manner of change, and a thing to be utterly despised. He indicates, too, that many inconveniences of body and chance befall us again and again on account of intemperance; and, on the other hand, that very many good things come our way through temperance.

Again, whatever befalls the perfectly ordered soul is dealt with so intelligently and borne so equably that no ill ever arises from it. But nothing within the body or outside it can be well ordered by the disordered soul.

In *Cratylus* he expounds the Greek word *sophrosyne* as 'temperance', the wholesome preserver of prudence. For he thinks that the glories of all true things have been born within the soul, and this is why a man who looks directly into himself will behold all true things within himself.

But he is prevented from looking within by immoderate feelings about the body and things bodily; whence it comes about that there is an initial need for temperance, through which the darkness of disturbances has been driven away, and the mind, becoming calmer, is bathed in the light of the divine Sun, thus regaining wisdom and then obtaining prudence. And so, since wisdom and prudence accompany temperance, Plato, in other dialogues as well as in this one, often intends wisdom and prudence to be included in the word 'temperance'.

However, Socrates advises Charmides to look back at himself if he wishes to speak about temperance, for such a turning to oneself is the specific function of this virtue; and anyone who has fully turned to himself will understand human temperance through the very idea of temperance that is innate to the mind, and then, acknowledging moderation itself, by which God has tempered the parts of the soul from the outset, will recognise why the emotion of the soul needs to be tempered.

Furthermore, he is indicating in his guidance that no one who is not tempered should, or can be persuaded to, speak about temperance. Moreover, it is related in the *Timaeus* that all things turn out well for us through a certain harmonious modulation of the soul both in relation to itself and in relation to the body.

Indeed, the Pythagoreans, whom the Roman Censorinus follows in this matter, promise unending health to the soul and body, provided that the soul carefully moderates each of its movements and each movement of the body; and both Censorinus and we ourselves have found that this was what befell very many wise and holy men.

Some attribute the longevity of the ancients to this very cause or a similar one; but, in addition, something even more amazing is that the sages promise immortality to bodies through their songs and poetry. In *Alcibiades* Plato says that the magic art of Zoroaster is nothing other than holy worship, and he adds that it is not only by songs of magic but also by principles of philosophy that the soul is tempered and the body is kept far from death for ever or at least for a long time.

Indeed, that speech which is intended to commend temperance in his hearers, and also to implement it, requires two things in particular: the power imparted by God, and the principles derived from the philosophers. And the speech composed of these two Plato calls the magical charm by which Phoebus, and later the Pythagoreans, miraculously drove diseases away from both soul and body.

It must not be considered wrong to say that the body can be rendered immortal when the soul is fully tempered and that the body falls into diseases and evils when the soul is untempered. For this is in the Mosaic mystery concerning the condition and fall of our first parent. And Avicenna, following the Platonists and Hippocrates, shows that the soul, by its very nature, transcends all matter to such an extent that as soon as it is restored to itself it can move the universal elements by some marvellous power and exercise control over all bodies; all the more control does it have, therefore, over its own body.

This is what Adam was able to experience initially; and some think that Enoch and Elias, for a similar reason, are still alive; and some believe that the same is true of the Evangelist. But we discuss all of these matters in great detail in our *Theology*.

Finally, to put it briefly, the marvellous power of temperance is manifest in the fact that it restores happily to itself the soul which has fallen unhappily upon things that are not so good as itself. Manifest, too, is the marvellous power of the soul from which all things good and bad flow forth upon the body and by whose will the body can be preserved incorruptible. This concurs in almost all points with the Mosaic mysteries.

Then the question 'What is temperance?' is put quite frequently and is never resolved by Charmides or by Critias. For Charmides puts forward not temperance itself but things which accompany temperance; while Critias puts forward things which pertain more to prudence, and even that he does inappositely; so that what is made clear is that it does not behove anyone to expatiate on such a noble virtue.

Meanwhile, we should take note that the priests in ancient times had the custom, in their rites, of consecrating the third libation-bowl especially to Jove the Preserver, making it clear, as Plato relates in the *Laws*, that the beginning, the middle, and the end of all things are ordered and maintained under the providence of Jove.

But let us return to the absurdities perpetrated by Critias, who says that there is a knowledge which knows both itself and all knowledges but does not know the very things which are the objects of those knowledges. This is absurd, of course, because truth itself and the principle of knowledge are within the very Self of those things which are known, as if through some contact and harmony. Moreover, knowledge cannot be perfectly known unless the nature of knowledge is appreciated; and there can be no such appreciation unless there is knowledge of individual things.

Again, Critias admits that anyone who does not know at all is able at the same time to know that he does not know. But Socrates does not accept this, because those things which are completely unknown cannot be known in any way. For whoever realises that he does not know something acknowledges that he is cut off from it. If this is his judgement, he has already delineated some idea about it within himself: the idea by which he deems himself cut off and by which he is cut off from that thing in particular. The result is that whoever recognises that he does not know something is not totally ignorant of it but defines it, I say, with a general outline, because within the specific differences among things lies the perfect knowledge which Plato seeks in all his discussions.

But when he shows Socrates acknowledging that he knows nothing, he is showing that he holds general, though not specific, definitions of things, for otherwise he would be unable to acknowledge his ignorance. For the same reason, as long as he knew nothing, in a way he knew everything. But since Critias had moved the conversation from temperance to prudence, and had done so by some kind of Platonic licence, Socrates states that prudence – the knowledge of good and evil – holds sway with respect to supreme bliss, because it reveals both a good end and good means to that end and because all things and all arts, provided that they are governed by prudence, lead us to the good, but certainly do not do so if they are not governed by prudence.

Finally, Socrates teaches that nothing is more difficult to define, or to acquire, than temperance. The difficulty of its definition arises from the fact that it is hard to differentiate it from the other virtues, with which it is in harmony, and from the additional fact that the greater the difficulty of inner possession the greater is the difficulty of understanding it and of expressing it in words.

Indeed, since it is from our dealings with the body that we are most inclined to slip into pleasure and intemperance, and since we have been nurtured in intemperance from our infancy, it is extremely difficult for us to acquire temperance. Besides, our first sensory impressions seem to contribute something to courage through anger and boldness; to prudence through fear; to patience through pain; and to justice and liberality through love.

But every movement is opposed at all times to temperance; for since temperance resides only in deep stillness, access to it from any direction is prevented by any kind of impulse. The difficulty is aggravated by the fact that, just as it is the hardest thing of all to find within the body a completely harmonious tempering of the humours and of the parts, it is likewise the hardest thing of all to find within the soul the harmonious tempering of all its parts.

For this reason Socrates is right, in the epilogue as well as at the beginning, to say that it is necessary to pursue temperance, which is very like celestial harmony and which is imparted by celestial and divine power to the soul, to principles, and to words. But on all occasions he admonishes us to strive to be made temperate through lawful ordinances rather than hold discussions about temperance on dialectical principles. For temperance is known only with very great difficulty, and once it is known it is of no benefit unless practised but becomes a very great obstacle; and, even more importantly, unless it is actually realised in practice, it cannot be known perfectly, for nothing impure can attain that which is purest of all.

Summary of *Laches*,
Concerning Courage

P LATO AGAIN and again puts the best magistrates above the laws, because without magistrates the laws seem to be quite useless, for no one will observe them; but the best magistrates are the laws. He says, however, that the best magistrates cannot appear unless the citizens are the best of men; and the men will not be the best unless the youths and the boys are also the best. For this reason, in almost all the dialogues, Plato exhorts parents to first bring up their children properly, for he knows that the human race cannot live honourably or be governed happily without the very best governors.

Moreover, there will never be good princes in the state unless they are the most upright of men, carefully nurtured right from their tenderest years. But since the regulation of childhood for the most part is quite often put into the care of servants, while youth, finding some licence and shaking off some of its fetters, strays hither and thither without restraints, our Plato is justified in putting his main emphasis on the need to correct and restrain young people.

He deeply deplores that period of life which combines insolence and pride with softness and licentiousness; and this is why it has been put in very great jeopardy, being too little under the watchful eye of the servants and being sadly overlooked by the laws and the magistrates, especially since the young people are universally contaminated by each other as seriously as they are infected by their elders.

In the *Laws* and the *Republic*, therefore, Plato appoints one magistrate to have specific charge of the youth. This magistrate – one might almost say that he resembles a bishop – should send out scouts every day and night throughout the city, to observe the habits, words, and actions of every single young person and to make a faithful report of all their deeds and words to the magistrate, as if to a shepherd and a father.

However, the needful care of the youth was not a cause of anxiety for Plato alone of all men; indeed, Aristotle himself could not refrain from giving the highest praise to Plato in this matter. But let us turn to the dialogue.

Lysimachus and Melesias are considering the education of their sons; they complain about their own fathers, who took too much care of managing public affairs and thus neglected their own households and their own sons. But since the foremost care of the state lies in caring for the youth, and since they intend, although now old, to consider these things in a more reasonable way, they call together Nicias and Laches, who are also old men and have sons of their own, to deliberate together on these subjects; and to ensure that the investigation has no deficiency they consult Socrates, not only as a friend but also as a judge, for throughout his life Socrates is concerned exclusively with the proper remedies for the youth.

But in the meantime you will be considering the wonderful praises bestowed upon the Socratic life, and you will deem that true praises are those which proceed from a man who is worthy of praise. Yet since in some states the institution of laws tends towards softness rather than boldness, while the reverse is true in other states, Plato considers both types to be dangerous and, in the *Statesman*, he requires softness to be combined in equal measure with boldness, and boldness to be combined with softness.

However, if anyone unites *Charmides* with *Laches*, he will be linking exhortation with temperance in the first instance, and with courage in the second instance, and he will rightly temper the hearts of the youths. I make but passing mention of the fact that, in the exhortation to courage that is in this present dialogue, both Nicias and Laches have rather too much admiration for military courage. Nicias, moreover, is extravagant in singing the praises of training in skill at arms as a most necessary preparation for warfare, but Laches justly corrects him.

After this it is time to hear Socrates' view. Note at this point that no harmony brings greater delight than the harmony found in a wise man, which arises from the harmony of mind and speech. On the other hand, no disharmony gives more offence than the disharmony of tongue and mind. Note, too, that a corrupt man, though he speak fine words, should not be heard. None but the moral should speak of morals.

Moreover, Socrates always had the habit, whatever the subject under discussion, of taking his partner in the debate to the point where he revealed the *raison d'être* of his whole life, the point being that it is futile to know anything unless you know yourself. It is also necessary first of all to submit to examination by someone else, to whom the reasons for the life lived hitherto are frequently imparted, a procedure which strongly supports the annual confession instituted by Christians. Again, one should learn all the time one is alive.

But Socrates, the most cautious of all men, says that the judgement which has been put into his hands should be transferred to his elders. In the meantime, however, being implored by everyone, he tackles the main subject, praising most highly the care given to educating one's children, while condemning carelessness in this matter. He adds that it is impossible for anyone to exhort another to be courageous unless he knows how to express what courage is.

Soon afterwards Laches, being asked what courage is, answers with some confidence that it is that virtue by means of which a man, without leaving his post, trounces the enemy. This is refuted on the grounds that a man who does what the Scythians do may vanquish the enemy by fleeing as much as by standing fast, and may be just as courageous. This is why Homer describes as courageous the man who knows when to be bold and when to be timid. A short while later he is attracted to any subject whatever by the victory of courage, as it befits the courageous man to vanquish not only terrors but also pains, passions, and pleasures. Hence a definition that applies to all these is being sought.

The reply given by Laches is that it is a kind of mental endurance. But since this is an inadequate definition, Socrates insists on adding that this endurance must be honourable and beneficial, which it will not be unless it is exercised with prudence. This is why he compels Laches to say that courage is, in fact, prudent endurance, for courage is something beautiful and good.

The next questions are 'What is endurance?' and 'In respect of what is it prudent?' In other words, 'On what subject or function is it centred?' Now when Laches is questioned in general terms as to whether courage is greater when boldness is greater, he makes the mistake of granting that this is so; and he further admits, prematurely, that in a man who, having no experience of a situation but recognising its danger, faces this situation, boldness is greater than it is in a man who approaches the situation after being prepared by experience, for the latter will act with greater caution and care.

Finally, Laches admits that courage is greater when boldness abounds or when there is a dearth of experience and prudence. In making such an admission, he is contradicting himself as well as

admitting what is false. For courage is something beautiful and beneficial, whereas boldness is imprudent, base, and harmful.

At this point we should take note of the well-known view held by
Socrates and Plato: A man is good in relation to those things of which
he has knowledge, and he is evil in relation to those thongs of which
he has no knowledge. Indeed, just as all mistakes in handling and
walking arise from the failure to see, so all the errors of mankind in
discriminating and acting are held by Socrates to arise from the failure
to understand. For when the leader himself is blind, or has poor eye-
sight, everything goes to rack and ruin.

Following Laches, Nicias defines courage as knowing what to fear
and what not to fear, and for what reason and to what extent these
things are to be feared or engaged with. At any rate, he calls courage an
attitude consistent with prudence in regard to what should be feared
and what should be engaged with; but he describes boldness devoid of
prudence as rash aggressiveness.

Socrates reasons against Nicias in the following way: Any
knowledge of anything is not only of things past, which have already
happened, or only of things present, which are happening now, or
only of things to come, which may happen for the best; but it is
the nature of this knowledge to understand all of these. And so, if
courage is the knowledge of daring and fearing in relation to the good
and evil things that will happen in the future, it is certainly also
the knowledge of those things as they are now, as well as the knowledge of those things as they used to be: in short, it is the knowledge of
them all.

It is therefore a universal virtue. But we were initially looking for
courage as some discrete part of virtue. This objection has been made
not so much to refute Nicias as to test him. But Nicias did not know
how to defend his definition.

Among the older people, Socrates, however, not wishing out of
discretion to disturb the learned man, pretends to be likewise ignorant
of the definition, and he exhorts them to join him in seeking for
themselves instructors in the virtues before professing any ability to
teach the youth; and in this way Socrates makes it clear that at all stages
of life the prime requisite is moral training and that this should be
learnt without shame-faced blushes.

But the definition of courage, which he is seeking here, and the
definition of temperance, which he is seeking in *Charmides*, are not
resolved in either of these dialogues, where his intention is simply to

exhort and to admonish; but they are resolved in the *Republic* and in the *Laws*.

But to speak briefly of courage and temperance together, as if they were siblings: Plato, in the *Phaedrus* and the *Symposium*, compares our life on earth to a journey, in which the direction is given by reason as if by a charioteer, while the higher and lower emotions are like twin horses, one white and one black.

And insofar as it is appropriate to our theme, let us make a clearer distinction: Divine providence, he says, has determined to call us away from what is base, and to spur us forthwith towards what is honourable; and likewise he says that modesty and magnanimity were implanted within us at our birth, so that our charioteer, being restrained by modesty as if by reins, will hold our affections, like horses, away from what is base, even though the base be sweet; and with the spurs of magnanimity he will urge us on towards what is honourable, even though the honourable be austere; for some evil daemon uses allurements to entice our desires towards what is base, and employs the bitterness of pain to deter us from what is honourable.

This is why temperance, applying the reins of modesty, causes us always to abstain from the base, contrary to the pull of pleasure; and this is also why courage, responsive to the spurs of magnanimity, takes care to ensure that we strive manfully towards what is honourable, despising the fear inspired by difficulty and pain. And the more difficult it is to transcend pain than to abstain from pleasure, the more difficult it might seem to anyone to put courage before temperance.

Finally, temperance ensures that we do not fall from the human condition into that of the brute; while courage further ensures that we somehow move into God, the Master of all. It was on account of this virtue that the whole of antiquity numbered Hercules among the gods: Hercules, I say, conqueror of the earth, who called out as he mounted the steps to heaven, 'Follow now, you men of courage, where the way of great example leads to heaven. Why show your backs in cowardly idleness? Earth, once transcended, grants access to the Stars.'

(Summary) of *Cratylus,*
Concerning the True Principle of Names

P LATONIC WISDOM always acknowledges the highest but never despises the lowest. However, the knowledge of true names is not low in the scale but high, especially when it is the knowledge of the divine names. *— Kaballah*

The wise men among the Hebrews esteemed this knowledge so highly that they placed it above all other forms of knowledge, and even above the written law, declaring that it had been imparted by God to the Patriarchs and to Moses; and it was Moses who would set it down, not in letters, but in the minds of holy men: in the minds of the Prophets who came after him and who later spread the wisdom of the divine names to the minds of those in the long line that followed. *In the "square letters" of "Chaldean."*

They therefore said that their forefathers had performed wonders *magic* through the power of these names and that they had put some of these names into their writings, but that these were, for the most part, scattered and obscure. If anyone can recognise and collect them and utter them perfectly and with the same purity of mind as that with which they were imparted to him, that man will likewise perform wonders, especially with the first name of God, which, being miraculously composed of only four letters, all vowels, can certainly not be rightly pronounced by anyone who is not divinely inspired. *joh he vaohe*

Hence they are obliged to admit that Jesus, whom they themselves call 'Nazarenus', was divine, since, indeed, they confess that he performed wonders through the true understanding and pronunciation of this tetragrammaton name. But we have spoken fully on these matters in our book *On Religion.*

Origen, too, after considering the miraculous power of the divine names and words, says in his books *Against Celsus* that wondrous power lies hidden in certain sacred names, and that this is why these names cannot be translated from the Hebrew tongue into any other but must be preserved in their own original characters.)?

95

Say: so far is F. from avoiding daemons that he brings them in unnecessarily just for an analogy!

For it may be that just as life endures in a body that is constructed on a particular principle, yet does not endure in one that is differently constructed or that is modified, so, they believe, a vital power is inherent in divine names that are composed in a particular divine way. And Hermes Trismegistus likewise taught in the beginning, as did Plotinus and Iamblichus long afterwards, that daemons are somehow enclosed within some statues that are constructed according to a particular design.

cf. p. 309

p. 130

But some gifts of God are bestowed by words which accord with a celestial pattern, and this happens by the providence of God, so that, whenever the situation requires it, we can rightly summon divine help.

magic

It is said that this was practised by Phoebus himself and by Pythagoras, who was reported to have miraculously cured mental as well as physical ailments by divine words alone. Herein, we have found, resides the entire wisdom of Zoroaster, which Plato in *Alcibiades* describes as divine and which in *Charmides* he calls the healer of the diseases of mind and body. *Zoroastrian magic works by div...*

omnific words

I merely allude to the fact that all peoples and tongues pronounce the special name of God with four letters only; for this subject is dealt *nam...* with at some length in our commentaries on the *Philebus*, where it is shown to have been impossible for all peoples to have concurred in this matter without being divinely inspired. Hence the Egyptians give the name 'Theut' to our 'Deus'; the Persians use the name 'Syre'; the Magi use the name 'Orsi', whence 'Oromasis'. The Hebrews, on all occasions, express the ineffable name of four vowels by saying 'Adonai'; the Greeks say 'Theos'; the Arabs say 'Alla'; Mahommed says 'Abdi'. We have received the name 'Jesus' from an angel.

in what trans? and contra suppose this but that's 5 letters! ck transl

sp? Jesu — same number

P/3

But why did God wish to be universally invoked by means of four letters? Perhaps because He Himself arranges all things on four levels: essence, being, power, and action. Again, the world of the heavens consists of the threefold nature of the four signs: fiery, airy, watery, earthy; and the world below the heavens consists likewise of these four elements.

? NO BU no, just the perception

But no one will wonder that such great power resides within true names, once we have considered that the natural power of anything, when we perceive it aright, moves from the objects to the senses, from the senses to the imagination, and from the imagination, in some mysterious way, to the mind. Next, it is initially conceived by the mind and then, like a child, it is expressed by means of a word. And within this word, which is composed of its own parts, the power of the

131D

131D Item Coelestia triplicatabus signorum quatuor, ignea, aërea, aquea, terrea, should transl: "the celestial [signs] are [in] four triplicities of the fiery [signs], the airy [signs]... triplic...

96

The power of a thing resides, like life, with form ? of its meaning

subject resides, like life, in the form of its meaning: I am speaking
of that life which is initially conceived by the mind itself through
the seeds of creation, which is later uttered through spoken sounds,
and which is finally preserved through writings.

If the names of all other things preserve the power of those things in
a certain way, and for this reason the things themselves are recognised
by means of those names, as if they were images of those things, how
much more do the divine names, being transmitted by God Himself,
preserve their own power for ever. And this is as it should be, for a true
name, as Plato would have it, is nothing other than a power of the thing
itself, being initially conceived by the mind, as I have said, then
expressed by the voice, and finally indicated by letters.

But for something divine the power must necessarily be divine. And
so, since divine power is inherent in the name of God, Plato directs us,
both here and in the *Philebus*, to honour them and, as he indicates in
the *Laws*, to honour them much more than even shrines and divine
statues. For the image of God is conveyed with greater clarity in the
artistry of the mind, especially if the mind is divinely inspired, than in
works made by hands.

Indeed, Plato considers the first and purest names of God to reside
within the celestial minds on high, by which, if I may express it thus,
God Himself is conceived more clearly. The second names are in the
purer daemons. The third names are in the souls of men, and these
names were proclaimed in ancient times, as if by trumpets, through the
mouths of men inspired by God. And in this way the names of God
that have been transmitted to us like images through the saints of old
appear to be rays of God Himself, passing through the higher divinities
and through the minds of holy men.

But anyone who looks upon the sun in wonder, as is only fitting,
necessarily honours the light of the sun, too. And thus it behoves us to
worship God first and to worship at the same time the rays of God: the
powers and images that are inherent in the meaning of the sacred
names.

Let us therefore listen to the words Socrates proclaims in the
Philebus: 'To me, reverence for the names of the gods is not an awe that
is human but an awe which surpasses even the strongest fear.' Let us
listen also to Socrates in the *Phaedrus*, as he confesses that he has
perhaps offended the name of God in his discussions on love. Let us
listen to Plato, in the eleventh book of the *Laws*, as he judges those
men to be utterly sacrilegious who have defiled the names of the gods

really? That's what he says p 1310

with lies and false oaths. He orders them to be slain by anyone without fear of reprisal, and he strongly condemns as a traitor to the laws anyone who, being present, does not punish such men.

On the other hand, we should not be troubled by his frequent references to many gods, for in *Parmenides* and the *Timaeus* he proves that God is Himself one, and that all others are the angelic and celestial servants of God. When he calls them 'gods', he means that they are divine rather than actual gods. But in the *Parmenides*, after he has connected everything to the one God, he does not consider that God's names should be rejected, for since the wondrous gifts of God are inherent in them it was right for that divine theologian, Dionysius the Areopagite, to diligently seek out all the mysteries of theology within the divine names.

e super-natural

But why have we passed over in silence that beacon of truth, Paul the Apostle? For he says that the word of God is living and effectual, cutting more keenly than any two-edged sword. He also says that God gave to Him 'a name which is above every name: that at the name of Jesus every knee should bow, of things in heaven, and things in earth, and things under the earth.'

? from Hebrews

But let us now return to the dialogue. Hermogenes, who is a disciple and follower of Parmenides, and Cratylus, a follower of Heraclitus, are in disagreement about the true nature of names. Hermogenes thinks that the power of names is purely arbitrary, whereas Cratylus thinks that their power has a natural basis. In the end, they submit themselves to the judgement of Socrates.

First of all, the three teachers of Plato here accord so beautifully with each other, for, apart from his own discoveries, Plato is said to have received moral training from Socrates, natural principles from Cratylus, and metaphysical teachings from Hermogenes in particular. Indeed, Cratylus is a follower of Heraclitus and of the other ancients who practised philosophy many centuries before Heraclitus and who considered that nothing anywhere is stable but that all things turn in perpetual motion, with the result that they usually gave things names based on motion.

Hermogenes, on the other hand, being a supporter of Parmenides and the Pythagoreans, maintains that all things remain steadfast.

Socrates and Plato arrange this dispute between Hermogenes and Cratylus in such a way that the view of Heraclitus needs to be tested in the natural sciences, while that of Parmenides needs to be tested in metaphysics; yet anyone who transfers the motionlessness of creation

= Bottom Op. p 1310 ok sit probanda S...
Parmenidis in metaphysicis set probanda S... mixtum transfer at

I cd crit. but it's a quibble.

to the natural world, or motion to the divine world, will meet with strong disapproval. *improbandus disproved*

But these things aside, Socrates seems to incline more towards the view of Cratylus concerning names, confirming it in the following way: One of the propositions is true, and the other is false; the parts of the true proposition are true, while the parts of the false proposition are false. But the parts of a proposition are names, which means that some of the names are true and some are false. The true proposition is that which states things as they are, while the false proposition does the opposite. It follows that the true names are those which declare things as they are, rather than in some arbitrary fashion.

Nod

But since Protagoras thinks that things are as they appear to any particular individual, with the result that nothing has its own essence, and human opinion is the measure of everything, Socrates argues, against Protagoras, that some men are excellent, by which he means very prudent, while others are very bad, meaning that they are far removed from prudence. And if, as Protagoras thinks, an individual's opinions are true for that individual, there will surely be no difference between the prudent man and the imprudent. *K mod thought*

But Protagoras is very ingeniously refuted in the book on *Knowledge*; yet it was necessary to briefly refute him here, too, so that the view of Hermogenes about names – a view in some respects similar to that of Protagoras – might the more easily be disproved. It is true that Hermogenes gives no credence to Protagoras' views on created things, but when he says that names hold the truth of things according to the judgements of men, he reveals his personal inclination towards the view held by Protagoras, and also towards the view of Euthydemus, who says that all things are always present to all people in a similar way, and who is summarily rebuked because there would be no good men and no evil men if virtue and vice were equally present to all.

But in this discussion note that our Plato holds the very widespread view that the whole power of virtue lies in prudence, while the whole power of vice lies in imprudence. *idea also endorsed 're knowledge; an easily in this*

After the view of Protagoras and Euthydemus has been refuted, the conclusion is reached that things themselves are what they are on account of their own nature in the order of creation and not on account of our opinion. For if essences exist naturally, then the actions performed and suffered are also natural. And so, if we are seeking to burn something, we shall succeed if we act in accordance with the nature of the object rather than by following our own whim, so that in this way *book con dicons.*

ansl

ta componunt, ut Herac99quidem sententia in physicis uis autem vel statum rerum ad naturalia, vel in divina, sit penitus IMPROBANDVS." 1510 bot

and with the means by which the object may be readily broken down we may break it down and burn it.

But speaking and naming seems to be an action and therefore it must have its own nature, so that we name something as its measure requires and not as it suits us. For name is an instrument by which we distinguish and differentiate the thing named from all others. But an instrument of this kind, as is obvious in the case of other instruments, must be fitted for its proper function, not haphazardly or by whim, but in accordance with art, so that through the very idea of art it receives that form which is conducive to the aim of making the most appropriate distinctions and differentiations. Such an instrument – a name – being equipped to distinguish things and also to teach any who hear it, is not for all and sundry to create, since to create it is the task of a craftsman, the establisher of names, who is the rarest of all men.

Now he creates names on the basis of what the craftsman who is going to make use of the names requires and intends. Such a man Plato considers to be the dialectician. But the man who creates in accordance with the idea of the object, the idea conceived by the mind, in which consists the true principle of the name, composes the name which is endowed with a definite meaning. And this ideal principle and meaning is the true name, and it remains the same in whatever form of letters it may appear, and among all peoples, provided that, through its distinctiveness, it teaches what the object itself is. You may draw the conclusion that, if names are to be true and are to be correctly set down, they must be framed by the wise establisher of names, and the dialectician must advise on the form they should take, so that they copy and develop as fully as possible the properties of the objects.

After this, when he is making a careful inquiry concerning those from whom the correctness of the names is to be learnt – that is, the properties which constitute the principle – he scorns the Sophists and directs us instead to the poets: not to the poets indiscriminately, but to the divine poets, as to men who have received the true names of things from the gods and whose writings contain the true names.

At this point he shows that Homer's poetry is allegorical, even when he seems to be relating history, as is evident in the names that are formed allegorically. He mentions many names of heroes in Homer's work, names that are composed on a definite principle of allegory; then he moves up to the names of the deities, taking the principles of the names from the more distinguished theologians.

100

At the first level of these names, 'Coelius' signifies the soul of the starry sphere, 'Saturn' signifies the soul of the following sphere, and 'Jupiter' signifies the soul of the third sphere.

At the second level, 'Coelius' means god, 'Saturn' means the angelic mind, and 'Jupiter' means the celestial soul of the world.

At the third level, 'Coelius' indicates the abundance of God Himself, 'Saturn 'indicates the intelligence of God, and 'Jupiter' indicates God's beneficent will that provides for all.

At the fourth level, 'Coelius' designates, within any divinity, a gaze directed towards the higher, 'Saturn' designates a gaze back towards oneself, and 'Jupiter' designates a gaze outwards to provide for all that is lower.

I shall be obliged to be more prolix if I wish to interpret each of the gods theologically, and indeed we have expatiated on this matter in our book *On Love* and in our *Theology*. But since a treatment of things divine is not the function of a man who always says that he knows nothing, Socrates conveniently says, whenever the consideration of divine matters becomes too profound, that that wisdom whereby he knows nothing has just begun to dawn, and in his way he indicates that divine inspiration is the prerequisite for true perception of the divine. He confirms this in the *Timaeus*, the *Symposium*, and the *Phaedrus*, and he demonstrates it in his *Letters*.

But when he says that he has received contemplation of the divine from Euthyphro, he is being ironical, for he scorns Euthyphro and the other ostentatious teachers of the divine law. The result, not unjustifiably, is that what he pretends to have heard from Euthyphro he shortly afterwards declares worthy of dismissal, and he warns us not to trust the teachings of ostentatious men, especially when they are deliberating on matters divine, about which even the most upright man is at all times unable to speak as a man, though he may on occasion speak as the trumpet of God. This is rather like the words of Plutarch when he says that among the Greeks there was a law which decreed that the books of wicked men, even if they were good books, should be destroyed, so that the memory of their authors would be effaced.

He also showed that the ancients followed the practice of using certain prayers and sacrifices to quickly release anyone who had been seized by a daemon in the course of the sacred ceremonies, thus preventing him from being over-wearied by the daemon.

He further teaches that it is not right to spend a long time on names.

He likewise reprimands those who think that only the world-spheres and the stars are divine, since, in fact, it is from those things which are changeable and closer by nature to our perception that the ascent may be made towards the higher divinities, which, being closer to perfection, are steadfast and beyond the range of our senses.

He tells us, in addition, that the names of the gods were not devised by chance but were devised partly by human reason and partly by divine inspiration. But the names of heroes and the names of men were often given on the basis of the ancestral family names or from personal choice, and this is why a definite principle is to be sought in the divine names rather than in any others.

He then moves down to the daemons and declares that, in the view of Hesiod and the ancients, the souls of the most upright men arise in the airy daemons, who are richly endowed with the wisdom of the creation and who provide for the human race. But take note at this point that every good man is a wise man and, again, that a good man becomes a wise man because God fills the purified, clear mind of the good man with the light of His wisdom. The wise man, in turn, is good because he does not stray from the aim and he makes no mistakes in selecting those things which are conducive to the aim.

Note that heroes and demi-gods are considered identical and that they are born from mutual love between God and man. Hence the saying 'But they are born of God'. Thus is demonstrated the relationship between the human race and the divine.

Now mark that the function of man is not to perceive, but to consider what he has perceived; next, that the function of the soul is not to be contained in the body but to contain the nature of the body, although Orpheus says that the body is the prison and tomb of the soul, so that, insofar as the soul is in the body, it is deemed to be dead.

Remember, too, that Anaxagoras considered the one soul of the created world to exist before all others, and he also considered the one mind to be pre-eminent. Hence his words: 'Spirit nourishes inwardly, and Mind, filling all the parts, moves the entire mass.'

Consider next the respectful discretion shown by Plato when he says, 'Whoever is wise acknowledges that he does not know the gods or the names that the gods use among themselves.' He adds that we should beseech God to reveal to us the name that is proper to Him, and that we should consider that the names which we give to God express our own ideas and feelings about God rather than His true nature. For this reason we should pray that we do not displease God with the names we give Him. The same thought is conveyed in *Philebus*, *Parmenides*, *Phaedrus*, and *Timaeus*.

He then expounds the names of the gods by presenting, initially, the views of those who believed everything to be in flux, views which he will finally reject.

But at this point remember that, in fact, the goddess Vesta signifies the essence of differentiated forms and the steadfast foundation of the divine world, and it was for these reasons that the ancients had the practice of sacrificing to Vesta before all other deities.

He says, furthermore, that the names which signify stillness in divine beings are related to their substance, while the names which signify movement are related to their action: they are wrongly related to intellectual action, but rightly related to physical action.

Again, he says that the masculine names of the deities indicate efficient action within the divine world, while the feminine names indicate potentiality.

Moreover, because heaven by its movements begets time, which continuously consumes, there is a particular image which shows Coelius the god and Rhea, together with Saturn, who is devouring his own children. Now Coelius is divine essence, Rhea is his life, and Saturn is his mind. The children of Saturn are the Ideas of things, born of the divine intelligence within them, which, being brought forth by mind, are returned to mind, which, if I may express it thus, absorbs them into itself.

But the hosts of deities which encompass the various parts of the world are held within the Ideas of those parts, as well as within the angelic minds which contemplate the Ideas in multifarious ways; and they are also held within the souls which rule over the spheres of the world and over the stars.

Mark especially that Pluto here signifies particularly the divine providence which pertains to differentiated souls and which employs the everlasting charms of its own good qualities to seize and hold the pure souls so firmly that they do not wish to return to us again. But because he does not accept the never-ending cycles which Plotinus and Proclus allot to souls, he shows that the souls in thrall to Pluto are fettered so tightly and inescapably because they are held by a feeling of love.

In the *Symposium*, the *Laws*, and in many other places, Plato confirms this view that the knot tied with love and willingness is more binding than all others; and he is right to do so, for the man who attracts another through desire, seizing him from within rather than from without, exerts a more powerful pull upon him and holds him with a stronger grasp than does the man who seeks to attract another through any other force.

Moreover, any who have been seized in this way, far from striving to be released, support themselves on the one who is binding them and entangle themselves even more tightly in the same chain.

I merely mention the fact that any other captor appears to be a stranger from a higher position; but the captor through love makes his way into our hearts both overtly and covertly, as if he were an equal and a member of the household.

Hence Boethius proves, from the philosophy of Plotinus, that God draws all things to Himself with the utmost power and the utmost gentleness, attracting everything with the bait of love for Himself, which is love for the Good. This is also confirmed by Philo, a follower of Plato.

From beginning to end God touches all things with His power and orders them with His gentle sweetness. We shall show elsewhere that all of this has been taken from the fourth book of the *Laws*. However, with regard to Phoebus, who, according to Orpheus, signifies the vital light, there are many excellent sayings in the Orphic *Hymn to Apollo*, in the sixth book of the *Republic*, and in the *Oration* of Julian the Platonist, as well as in our little work, *On Light*.

But for the moment the name of Apollo is explained briefly as signifying the threefold sun: divine, angelic, celestial. In the first, it is the light above the intellect; in the second, it is the intellectual light, which is above sight; in the third, it is visible light. The second is called 'the first-born' by followers of Plato. The third is said to be a reflection of the first two.

But to speak briefly: Apollo signifies, firstly, the simplicity of the divine and angelic substance; secondly, the power by which God and the angelic hierarchy wash the souls and cleanse them of their lower inclinations; thirdly, the grace by which they release them from what is worse and unite them with what is better; fourthly, the skill, if I may put it thus, of the archer, by which they shoot his gifts upon all things far and wide, though they afflict the unjust with his barbs; fifthly, the efficacy which tempers and changes all things through the modes of music.

Here we can see the prophecy of Apollo, when it is described as pure and simple, washing and releasing through cleansing. Here we can recognise the healing art and the skill of archery and song, when he puts forth his powers upon all things, gently tempers all things, and happily turns them back to himself through the fullness of temperance. Such gifts and effects are also perceived in the sun and in the third and celestial aspect of the sun.

This is where Socrates says that he is jesting in his exposition of the names of the gods, meaning that he understands that he is not reaching the divine substance through these names but is explaining, as best he may, the effects they produce or our feelings about the gods. He adds that the gods, too, occasionally jest and sport. We jest about the divine, and the gods jest about the human, for our affairs are of minimal import to them, while they, for their part, govern human affairs without the least strain and, in fact, with unimaginable ease.

At this point I shall simply mention these words of Plato: 'Man is the plaything and sport of the gods', which I shall expound when the time requires it.

Next, and thirdly, the strictly religious man says that he fears to speak further about the gods. At the very beginning of the discussion there was some reason to be afraid of speaking about God without due acknowledgement of God; and again, in the central part of the discussion, it was right to be afraid of arrogantly seeking to measure the immeasurable; and then, towards the end, there was good reason to fear taking our discussion about names further than the will of the gods inspires us to do.

Now note that the full power of Mercury is concerned with speech, and appreciate that the power of understanding belongs to Saturn. Again, he adds that Pan, the son of Mercury, has a two-fold form because the twin aspects of speech are the true and the false; note that when Pan is depicted as a man he represents true speech and when he is depicted as a beast he represents false speech. The intention is that, after such a warning, you should be afraid of speaking what is false, lest by speaking what is false you become a false man and a true beast.

In the same way, when he scorns many of the ancients because as long as they suffered from giddiness they thought that everything was spinning around, he is warning us against measuring the eternal by the standards applicable to our nature, especially our temporal nature.

Again, when he says that temperance is the resort and abode of prudence, he is showing us that the soul which is intoxicated by the agitations of the body is unable to perceive the truth of things, especially of things incorporeal.

When he proceeds to interpret the name of the good, he is making it clear that three things are true of the Good itself: it is to be marvelled at; it is to be loved; it is sweet. It is to be marvelled at when it arouses us, diverts us from other things, and turns us to itself. It is to be loved when we move towards it and cleave to it. It is sweet when we are filled with it.

Shortly afterwards, in expounding the name of justice, he teaches us that the divine judgement pervades all, as Orpheus proclaimed in his hymns. He then points out that for the followers of Anaxagoras justice is the goddess who orders the minds of all.

Socrates dares not affirm this or deny it. He does not deny it because justice is an attribute of God; and he does not affirm it because it would be more appropriate to say that justice is the divine will which allocates all things in accordance with the merits of their nature or intention.

Note that the principle of the Good is a property of nature, which pervades all things, while the principle of the beautiful is a property of wisdom and order, emanating from itself and calling all things back to itself. Finally, note that the power of love is related to an influence from the eyes which penetrates through the eyes.

On the subject of names, he then says many things which can be quite well understood from what has gone before. He touches on the three-fold view concerning the origin of names: that they were received from the gods in former times; that they were given by barbaric peoples; or that through the passage of time since their origin they have been so greatly modified that their initial forms can no longer be discerned.

He goes on to reject those who profess a knowledge of what will come, when they do not know what has gone before. But mark this golden statement in what he then says: 'The most serious deception of all is that by which man deceives himself; for in such deception the deceiver is never separate from the deceived.'

But because Cratylus inclines towards the followers of Euthydemus, who thinks that no one utters falsehood since anyone who speaks says what is and therefore speaks the truth, Socrates dismisses this view in the following way. We often say that things which are far away are present to someone and, on the other hand, that things which are present are not present, and that this is nothing other than uttering falsehood. In the same way, we may use an appropriate name and thus express, through the name and through the sounds of the letters, something of the nature and the activity or passivity of the object; or we may use inappropriate names.

Later, when he is referring to numbers and qualities, he says that in the sequence of numbers the magnitude of the number is changed by the addition or subtraction of unity, which is not the case with regard to its quality. In my view, this happens because the whole principle of number consists in unity and its reduplication; whereas with regard to quality, since it is by nature beyond unity and its reduplication, the quality is not affected by the addition of subtraction of one or more steps.

It is the same with an image: for whether the image be large or small, its quality depends on its powers of representation. And it is exactly the same with names: for they are images of the things themselves.

Moreover, since the purpose of a name is to represent the thing itself, it is better to represent it through some similarity with the thing than to represent it through human convention. Again, since a name consists of letters, it cannot properly express the object unless it is composed of syllables and letters which aptly express the object. But since it is an arduous task to bring letters, syllables, and names into full conformity with individual objects – in fact, it cannot be done with countless objects – it is necessary to combine the ways of nature, so that, as far as possible, the nature of the objects holds the authority of the names. But where it is impossible or extremely difficult to do this through the intrinsic nature of the object, it may be done through human custom and convention, either in isolation or in conjunction with nature.

Next, note the extreme care that must be given to principles, and the great discussion needed to establish them. Again, to approach knowledge by a route that is full of deception, as Cratylus warns, is to look for the qualities of things on the basis of their names, for the framer of the names has established the names, not in accordance with the things themselves but as he himself, not being subject to deception, thought fit.

Furthermore, different people can interpret the same names in different ways and can deduce contradictory meanings with equal probability. Indeed, many names have been given which suggest that things are in flux, while many others suggest that things are permanent. It is therefore quite erroneous to judge things on the basis of their names.

Next, consider the following: the man who first named the objects knew them before he named them. Again, consider the view held by the ancients, which maintains that a divine power instructed man from the beginning and taught him the names of things. This is in accord with the views expressed in *Protagoras* and the *Statesman*. For it was not possible for the human race, either from the beginning of the world or after catastrophic floods, to be instructed except by God.

But because Socrates says that he dreams about Ideas, he makes it clear that he is often made fun of both publicly and by the comic writers, and that the awareness of Ideas, through detachment of the mind, is considered similar to prophecy imparted in a dream.

Then he proves the existence of Ideas by stating that above imperfect forms there must be perfect ones. Again, Ideas are invariable, since type-principles and type-definitions always persist unvaryingly. He adds that if stillness were totally removed from things the result would be that nothing would really be one thing or another and nothing would be known, for at every moment it would deceive the one who is seeking to give a verdict and necessarily turn him into a false witness; moreover, there would be no consciousness, that is, no particular Idea of consciousness which persists without variation.

His conclusion is that the knowledge of things is to be sought, not from names, but from Ideas, whose concepts have been imparted to us as the first true names of things.

Finally, he warns young people not to make a quick and easy judgement about serious matters, but to go through a long process of learning and to wait for their more mature years before making their judgement.

Summary of *Gorgias*

S INCE TWO THINGS – consciousness and emotion – wield the greatest power in the soul, the Sophists, under the guise of truth, divert men's consciousness towards what is false, while the popular poets, using the bait of harmonious pleasure, frequently hurl the emotions into inharmonious upheavals. Lastly, the popular declaimers deceive men's understanding with their false notions and drive human emotions into multifarious activities.

For this reason, since it is through the assiduity of these people that the minds of men are made to grow sickly through false opinions and harmful emotions, Plato, the physician of men's souls, draws us, quite unreservedly, far away from the Sophists and also, to some extent, from orators and poets. Indeed, he banishes all Sophists, wherever they are.

However, he does not ban all poets, but merely those who fabricate disgraceful accounts of the gods and those who are keen to repeat and recount the agitations in men's souls; and these he does not ban from every place, but from the city, that is, from the crowds of the young and ignorant who are easily inclined to become agitated and to fail to appreciate the allegorical meanings intended by the poets.

And so, in the books of the *Republic*, he orders poets to be expelled or to be obliged to speak honourably about God and not to keep exposing their hearers to agitations, but to sing sacred hymns and to make serious presentations of the laws received from their forefathers and from the deeds of great men.

But to go back to the orators: Plato does not reproach all of these, either, but only those who assiduously apply themselves to persuading their hearers of anything they please, without any reason or discrimination, whether it be something bad or good, a false principle or a true one, or whether it be rhetoric to excite compassion or stir sedition, or rhetoric based on conjecture.

Such was the main theme put forward by Lysias of Thebes, and by Tisias, as well as by Gorgias of Leontini. But in the *Phaedrus* Plato puts

Pericles and Isocrates before all the others, because they combined eloquence with philosophy. And he adds that the true orator is required to understand the principles of things, the laws of traditional customs, the powers of words, and the nature of talents, and to compose a speech on a definite principle which is fashioned, as far as is possible, to suit the capacity of his hearers, for the sake of persuading them of the common good, and not with the aim of ensuring that what he says is pleasing to men rather than acceptable to God.

But he denounces as the greatest scourge of the state the man who, like Tisias and Gorgias, does not pursue truth and justice but follows popular opinion, which has merely the appearance of truth and probability, as if to say that eloquence without wisdom is a sharp sword in the hands of a madman. He castigates two above all others: Lysias in the *Phaedrus* and Gorgias in this present dialogue; for the greater their authority, the greater the danger they pose.

Polus, the orator and the follower of Gorgias, is hauled into court, and so is Callicles, their accomplice. But at first Socrates speaks through the mouth of his friend Chaerephon, against Polus, and then he speaks on his own behalf against Gorgias. But since these two were in the habit of making astounding boasts in public about identifying the principles of everything in the world, he shows, with the intention of removing all their credibility, that they do not know how to adduce the principles of their own profession.

For when Polus is asked what the art of Gorgias is, he should have defined it purely by its essentials and explained what it is, but instead he skirts around the subject with non-essentials; and its nature is asserted in the exaggerated style which he typically employed in the *Phaedrus* when dealing with the styles of the orators. Then Gorgias himself, on being asked what his art is, replies with crude ostentation that it is rhetoric. He is subsequently asked to define rhetoric.

But we must remember that anything, inasmuch as it is itself, concurs in part with other things and in part differs from them; and that that through which it concurs is conventionally called 'kind', while that through which it differs is called 'difference'. Thus the definition which comprises the thing itself must be based on its kind and on its distinctiveness.

Gorgias, therefore, being someone who does not know how to define his own art, suggests its kind, and even that he does in a clumsy way. But it is only after much questioning and probing by Socrates that he is eventually and reluctantly compelled to admit the distinctiveness which he should have admitted at once in the first answer, side by side with kind.

His first answer is that rhetoric is the art concerned with discourse. But since there are other arts that are similar, he is asked to be specific about this discourse and its nature, so that it may be seen in what respects rhetoric differs from these other arts. His answer, however, is that rhetoric is about discourse, which provides the power of speaking.

But since this, too, is common to many arts, he is once again goaded into adding that rhetoric deals with discourse about things of the greatest import. Yet since this, too, is common, he is now compelled to adduce something more specific, to the effect that through oratory it comes about that we serve no one but we master others, and that oratory is the effective art of persuasion through domination.

Socrates, however, directs us in our discussions to give heed not to the person with whom the discussion is taking place but rather to the subject itself, to the words, and to the intention. But since all art persuades us of something, the next question is: What is the persuasive art of the orator concerned with, and what is the nature of his art?

The art of persuasion is at once divided into two aspects: that which leads to knowledge and that which leads to belief. The conclusion reached is that the persuasive art of the orator leads not to knowledge but to belief, not in relation to any subject whatever but in relation to matters of justice; not in all places but in a crowd most of all; and particularly concerning state affairs. Indeed, it is added that the orator can speak more persuasively on matters that truly pertain to other arts than can the practitioners themselves, although this is not in the presence of those who are experienced in these arts, but in the presence of the inexperienced.

At this point, let us heed the warning never to make wrong use of power and art and not to be troubled in debate, where serenity is essential for the perception of truth. Again, refutation should be accepted with a calm and joyful heart, especially when ways of living are being corrected, for there is nothing worse than perceiving false elements in our ways of living.

Gorgias subsequently concedes that the function of the orator is not to know how things are, but to devise a method of being so persuasive that he himself, although ignorant, seems to understand better than those who actually know; it is his duty to speak vigorously in public about anything, not by teaching but by persuading. He further concedes that the orator can and must know what is plausible, though he may not know what is true, a situation that cannot possibly occur; for if you do not know the thing itself you will never know what is similar to it.

In the same way, there is the question as to whether the orator, having no need to know anything else, needs to understand what is good, what is honourable, or what is just. But although Gorgias has said elsewhere that the orator stands in relation to these things as he does to the earlier ones, he here contradicts himself and agrees that he should know these things at least.

Hence Socrates reasons that if the orator knows what is just he is a just man. In this way he tests Gorgias, to see if he will hold to the necessity of this conclusion. Gorgias, for his part, admits at once that, since this is the proper conclusion according to the sciences and arts related to understanding, 'He knows the elements of astrology, or at least the mechanics; and so he is an astrologer, or at least a craftsman'.

However, in matters relating to the will and to ways of living, it does not follow that 'He knows what is just and he is therefore a just man'. For justice needs the will. Nevertheless, if anyone has divine knowledge of justice, which is what Plato says can happen sometimes under the inspiration of God, then that conclusion will rightly follow. For all who know beyond peradventure how great a good justice is and how great the benefit is that accrues from it, and who know, conversely, how great an evil injustice is and how great the suffering is that results from it, will undoubtedly flee from injustice and embrace justice.

Whichever way things are, Gorgias is forced to contradict himself. Indeed, although he has conceded earlier that the orator can be unjust on occasions, he now denies it. Then, starting from the arrogance of Polus, Socrates uses irony to arraign the younger men if they ever batten upon older men in a spirit of arrogance, and he advises them all to readily allow themselves to be corrected by anyone.

Now, in order that what follows may be clearly understood, it must be noted that rhetoric may be considered either in its kind or in its types: in its kind, it is defined as that diligence which is fully ready to be persuasive in any civil matter, whether it be by its ability to test and prove or, most of all, by the grace of its eloquence. And it is for this reason that rhetoric has been established as the art of debating and the art of poetry. To this extent rhetoric is good for the intellect, but to the will it is neither good nor evil.

But there are two types of rhetoric: the first is philosophical, while the second is popular or sycophantic. The first is good, and the second is evil. The aim of the first is to guide the hearers to the common good through assured principles of things, words, and customs. This is the type to which he gives the most fulsome praise in the *Phaedrus*, the type composed of philosophy and serious poetry. The aim of the second type, however, is to produce whatever it fancies, through the plausible surmises of the masses and the passions of the heart. We assign this type to a place between sophistical poetry and vulgar poetry, it being compounded of these two and being the one that he denounces in this dialogue.

Now he divides the arts that are truly therapeutic for man into two principal kinds: the first kind heals the soul, while the second kind heals the body. With regard to the soul, he says that the power of law, which dispenses laws and moderates customs, moulds and establishes the soul itself in a fashion conformable to nature, while the judicial art restores the soul if it ever happens to fall from its position.

With regard to the body, he says that there are also two arts which are therapeutic for the body: the art of gymnastic, which directs the exercising of the body and does its best to strengthen it with good practices; and the art of medicine, which restores lost health to the body.

And so gymnastic in relation to the body is equivalent to the power of law in relation to the soul; and medicine in relation to the body is likewise equivalent to the judicial art in relation to the soul.

All of these he calls arts because they lead to the Good through a definite principle. He says that there is a subordinate nature or knowledge which is sycophantic, servile, and deceptive, and which copies these four arts in a deceitful way. Through the sophistical art it emulates the art of law; through common rhetoric it feigns the judicial art; through the art of painting it portrays the art of gymnastic; and through the culinary art it represents medicine.

However, he denies the name of art to the whole of this kind of sycophancy, because it does not lead to the true Good through a definite principle, but leads to pleasure through pandering. But anyone who may think that Plato, who is by far the most eloquent of all, is comparing eloquence to cooking, should read the *Phaedrus*, in which he shows his approval of eloquence by speaking in the simplest terms of its aim, its function, and its directions, and by asserting its similarity to medicine.

But since Polus extols the force of rhetoric and says that orators have the greatest power because they are able, if they wish, to commit their adversaries to prison, condemn them to death, strip them of their

113

possessions, or exile them from the city, Socrates shows with two lines of reasoning in particular that the unjust have no power at all.

The first line of reasoning is that power must needs be chosen as something good for each person who chooses; but it is clear that licence for unjust men, who are the prisoners of their own intentions, to do whatever they want, far from being good for them, is evil and, in the long run, harmful to them. Next, 'the greatest power is to be able to do whatever you wish.' But it is obvious that all men desire the true Good, although evil people never enact or pursue the true Good. He adds that the evil mind, simply because it is evil, is considered to be at variance with itself and insane and already dominated by sense-impressions.

Who, therefore, would say that a mind which is a weak and foolish slave to its own servants is mistress of those servants? However, all human qualities are of three types: the good, the bad, and the intermediate. Of the good qualities, the first is wisdom; the second is a desirable condition of the body; and the third is an adequate measure of good fortune. But the last two of these three are deemed good to the extent that they offer the mind fitting service. Their opposites are said to be evils; and the intermediate qualities are indifferent, not inclining more to good than to evil, such as the actions of going, sitting, and the like.

Moreover, no man wills either the evil or the intermediate, or what he is actually doing: in fact, he wills only the good and those things for whose sake he acts and is acted upon. Therefore men who do harm do not will harm itself but the good, for whose sake they act. But they do not attain the good, and thus they do not obtain what they will, and thus they have no power.

Next, taking his opportunity from the error that Polus shares with many others, Socrates transmits to us words of holy guidance: The man who is at liberty to commit grievous sins is close to being wretched; the man who actually commits grievous sins is already wretched; and the man who does not pay the penalty for his sins is even more wretched.

We should choose to bear ills rather than inflict them. The liberty to do whatever we like is not power, unless it is going to be of ultimate benefit to us. But it will be of benefit only to those who use it justly. The unjust, even if they wield power over the whole earth, are unhappy – indeed, they are most unhappy. For the greater their freedom to sin and not to pay the penalty for their sin, the unhappier they are considered to be. Happiness is founded on wisdom and justice; unhappiness, on their opposites.

But since the verdict of truth, which must be related to the stature of the judge rather than to the number of those making the judgement, resides, according to Polus, in the sheer number of witnesses, Socrates replies that the best way to make a judgement is to call into court a single witness, an adversary convinced by reason; for if a crowd of witnesses is herded together from all directions, it will have little bearing on truth.

Moreover, because Polus says that it is somewhat disgraceful to inflict harm, but worse to suffer it, Socrates takes issue with this and asserts that in human affairs and customs the good and the beautiful or honourable are the same, and that the evil and the disgraceful are also the same. Then suppose that the beautiful is evaluated for its desirability or its usefulness or both, while the converse is applied to the disgraceful. From this point he reasons thus: if it is more disgraceful to inflict harm than to suffer harm, not because it is more troublesome but because it is more injurious, and if it is therefore deemed worse, he at once adds that one must entrust oneself to reason for a cure, as if to a doctor.

He also states that the just punishment for sins is particularly beneficial to the one who is punished. For if this punishment is just it will also be beautiful and honourable, and therefore good. If it is good it will benefit the soul as medicine benefits the body, and, much more importantly, it provides release from the disease of the soul, which is the most serious of all diseases and ills.

Pay heed at this point to the view of the theologians that nothing is more necessary and more useful to sinners than to confess their sins, be moved by repentance, ask the judge for penance, and bear it with equanimity, so that the soul might be purged, before its incurable disease departs.

Next you will hear that it is extremely easy for us to speak of our own state to someone afflicted by a similar condition; that Socrates, being captivated by the love of Philosophy, always complies with this love; and that it is better for everything to clash with us than for the soul to be at odds with itself. Accordingly, when Callicles corrects Socrates for being too keen on subtleties, understand that the Sophists, in the person of Socrates, are being refuted by Plato.

Then Callicles touches upon the common view held by Thrasymachus and many others, who say that customs and laws are not based on the order of nature but solely on the opinion and imagination of men, a view refuted in the books of the *Republic* and in what now follows.

But understand that the charges which Callicles levels against philosophers are not aimed at true philosophers, but are aimed partly at the most dispirited of the Sophists and partly at those who misuse the study of philosophy when they follow logic alone, thus abandoning the other aspects of speculation; or when they batten upon speculation alone, thus ignoring the philosophical precepts of tradition and the civil institutions. However, within Callicles' invective some untruths are spoken which will be refuted later.

But the advice given next is to take all care in examining and testing our own soul and to choose as a judge that one in whom there is right discernment of the subject under discussion, together with goodwill, which allows a happier deliberation to be made, and, most of all, boldness, which removes all fear of expressing what he thinks will be beneficial.

Then Socrates advises us, since we are rational by nature, not to live under irrational chance and fortune, but with the utmost care to set a specific aim to our life and to select the most appropriate means of achieving that aim.

Finally, while he frequently begs Callicles to refute him unrestrainedly and boldly, he advises that nothing should be sought more earnestly than the medicine of the soul. At this point Callicles concedes that the more powerful and stronger are by nature the same as the better; and he says that natural justice wishes the man who is more powerful to possess all the property of those who are lower and to rule over them. He says that the law of that man is naturally just.

To this Socrates replies that if the more powerful and stronger and better are identical, and if a multitude is stronger than one person, then the multitude is also better and more powerful. Thus the laws of the multitude, being better and more powerful, will be naturally just. But the laws of the multitude decree that it is just for equality for all to be observed, and that it is more disgraceful to inflict harm than to suffer it. For this reason, not only is it ordained by law that it is more disgraceful to inflict harm than to suffer it, and that it is just to observe equality, as Callicles had said earlier, but the same is also ordained by nature herself.

Moreover, because Callicles had previously considered the more powerful men to be those who outdid all others in craftiness, boldness, and violence, Socrates corrects him step by step and compels him to admit that the man who is more powerful is the one who shows greater prudence and courage in governing the state.

Socrates also demonstrates at this point that he invariably draws the same conclusions from the same data, giving his approval to consistency and his disapproval to fickleness.

Callicles, however, now seeks to move beyond prudence and courage and towards temperance. But just as he previously went astray with regard to justice and power by following Thrasymachus, so now, by following Aristippus, he also goes astray with regard to temperance, calling it the stupid cowardice of the servile mind and asserting that virtue and happiness consist in titillating and sating the pleasures of the senses.

Socrates, on the other hand, at once girds up his loins to prove that temperance is not based on human opinion but on the order of nature. Indeed, the natural order requires the lower parts of the soul to obey the higher parts. It requires the entire soul to be in harmony in all respects with itself, to be healthy, and to be beautiful; not to act futilely but to pursue the designated aim. Such is the character and life of the temperate man. In the intemperate man, by contrast, reason, which is his queen, becomes the slave to servile lust, full of discord and listlessness, struggling to accomplish the impossible and sparing no effort in the pursuit of fleeting pleasure.

All of this Socrates expounds in the views particularly of the Pythagoreans Philolaus and Empedocles, using the twofold method of story and example, whereby it is to be considered that the soul, being wholly within this body, is indeed dead; that, being intemperate, it is condemned to the lower world, where it is wretchedly distressed by vain and unremitting toil, as it unceasingly struggles, with the leaky vessel of depraved and deceptive judgement, to fill the vessel of insatiable lust with the water of debauched delights.

Then, because Callicles bases happiness, as well as virtue, on the continual fulfilment of desires, and because he affirms that pleasure and the Good itself are identical, and that pain and evil are identical, Socrates puts forward a number of reasons to refute this view.

The first reason makes it clear that pleasure is not the Good itself, since pleasure is often very base and is found in the basest of men.

The second reason makes it clear that good and evil, being opposites, cannot exist in the same person at the same time. Yet pleasure and pain do exist in the same person at the same time, as when a thirsty person is drinking, for in that situation the discomfort of being thirsty coincides with the pleasure of drinking.

The third reason makes it clear that good and evil, as is the case with other opposites, do not depart from the same person at the same time, whereas pleasure and pain do depart from the same person at the same time, as when someone who is drinking puts an end, by the very act of drinking, to both the thirst and the delight at the same time.

The fourth reason makes it clear that each person is made good by the presence of the good, and is made evil by the presence of evil. Dissolute men, however, are not made good by the presence of pleasure, and evil men are not made upright by pain. Indeed, since good men and evil men often rejoice and suffer in equal measure, and sometimes the evil ones rejoice more while the good ones suffer more, it must be the case that if pleasure were in fact good and pain were evil, then it would follow that on many occasions both good men and evil men would be equally either good or evil, and sometimes good men would be more evil than even evil men, and evil men would sometimes be better than good men.

At this point take note that the direction given by Socrates needs to be observed: do not rush to the weightiest matters until you have pursued the lighter ones. Then some of those reasons are adduced to confirm that pleasure is not the Good itself, since there are many pleasures which are evil, harmful to both soul and body, and which distract us from what is best; for if pleasure were the Good itself, there would be no evil pleasure.

In the same way, the faculties are also distinguished, and those such as the arts move towards the good and the useful on a definite principle; while those which are forms of flattery seek pleasure alone, with no principle of true goodness in evidence; and among these he numbers poetry, music, and common rhetoric.

But in the discussion note this maxim: the strength and health of the body is based on a certain order and preparation, and in the same way the strength and health of the soul is based on order and preparation. From this it comes about that just as the virtue and vice of the body do not reside in opinion but in whether there is harmony with nature or opposition to nature, so the virtue and vice of the soul are not judged by the opinion of men but by the law of nature.

In the end, the conclusion must be drawn that insofar as it is naturally better to have a healthy body than a sick body, so it is better to possess a temperate soul than an intemperate soul. In what follows, this is also confirmed by the Pythagorean maxim that temperance in all matters is best.

Temperance is the most important thing of all to convey to young people, for it is through this that the excesses of childhood are corrected and the entire soul is tempered; and Socrates holds that it is soon followed by the other virtues, since the temperate man conducts himself well before God and men, and is dutiful, just, and courageous.

Then the conclusion is: Happiness resides in virtue alone, misery in wickedness alone, and all human affairs must of a surety be referred to virtue as their standard.

Moreover, just as virtue is essential to the attainment of bliss, so chastisement and punishment must be applied to vices, being remedies for the ills of the soul. In short, the intemperate man cannot be a friend to others, or to God, or to himself.

But to show us the natural excellence of temperance he adds, from the thoughts of the Pythagoreans and the followers of Orpheus, that the universe is held together by temperance, and also by harmony and justice, which are themselves embraced by temperance; and this is why, as Pythagoras says, intemperance in all things must at all costs be avoided like the plague.

But since equality in particular is common to both temperance and justice, he directs us to first observe equality, which he declares to be of the utmost importance for gods and for men; I mean geometrical equality, which allows equal distribution to be made to each in such a way that it is in just accord with each one's capacities and merits, being neither more nor less than is deemed needful for the capacity or the merit.

Of course, geometrical equality is based on right proportion, while arithmetical equality is based on having the same number on both sides. But these two types of equality are not identical. For the excess of six above four and the excess of four above two are equal in the eyes of the arithmetician, who considers numbers, since the excess is two in both cases; but they are unequal in the eyes of the geometer, the judge of proportion, for six exceeds four by the sesquialtera proportion, in which the larger number contains the whole of the smaller number together with one half of the smaller number. But four exceeds two by the double proportion.

By this kind of equality – which does not follow the method of numbering by giving as much weight to the one as to the other, but which follows the method of measuring by assigning to each neither more nor less than what is fitting for it – all things, he says, are preserved, for in this is held the justice of God in all His works and of man in his dealings with others, since in both cases it is apportioned according to the measure of his capacity and merit.

Having said this, he now declares that the theological foundations of morals are confirmed by unshakeable principles, especially the view that it is worse to inflict harm than to suffer it and the view that the worst thing of all is not to pay the penalty for an offence you have committed, for paying the penalty is like taking the medicines which would free the soul from injustice, the worst disease of all. For no greater harm can be conceived than that inflicted on the soul by vice; and just as it is not expedient for a man with a totally sick body to live, so it is not expedient for a man with a vice-ridden soul to live.

Again, it is virtue, rather than life in the body, that should be valued highly; and it is better to be killed by profligate men than to show that one is akin to them by behaving as they do. At this point he warns us not to try to tackle anything of which we have no experience, especially matters of some import, and public matters least of all.

But he utterly despises rhetoric if it is unable, either privately or publicly, to impart health to the soul but has regard merely to the body and to the things of the body. He derides even those who, while holding the helm of government, have always embellished the state with things that are superficially good and have failed to fashion the souls of the citizens with temperance and justice, although such a work is the only function of the true helmsman. And he concludes that helmsmen who have their eyes on the benefits of fortune rather than on the benefits of the soul not only fail to be of service but are actually very harmful to the state.

Besides, all the power and wisdom of a man depend on his keeping his soul undefiled from sins against God or men. For a very slight detriment to this life is a very serious detriment to eternal salvation.

Again, to help you to understand what Plato declares with regard to future rewards for virtue or future punishments for vice, you should know that, in Plato's writings, Saturn is taken to be the higher intelligence, in which are found the universal law for all things and the providence which embraces the essences of all things as well as the modes and orders of all forms.

Beneath this intelligence are three particular orders of divinities, to which the providence of Saturn assigns three specific functions. Those divine powers which serve to allot essences are known by the general name of Jupiter; those which aid in the distribution of lives are given the name of Neptune; and those which help to arrange the orders of forms receive the name of Pluto. Prometheus is the name given at one time to the level of divine powers which is below these three and which, especially in this life, assigns a formal order to a nature that is simply rational.

Finally, Plato intends the three sons of Jupiter – the judges of Asia, Europe, and Africa – to be understood as the three divine powers which serve Jupiter and Pluto in their main function of ensuring that the established order of justice is fulfilled in souls now separated from their bodies.

Take note, however, that the divine law washes away the removable stains of vice by fixed terms of punishment, but it prescribes everlasting punishment for stains that are indelible. This appears to argue against the unending transmigration of souls through physical forms. But his earlier statement, that the judges have erred in their judgement of the living, shows us two things.

The first is that it is not divine judgement, but human judgement, that is mistaken with regard to virtue and vice. The second is that divine providence intuitively perceived that judgements would be wrong if the living were judged by other men living in this physical form; and this is why it decreed that judgement should be made after this life, not on a particular occasion, as the saying goes, but in eternity.

Remember, too, that the soul carries with it the characteristics and the habits of vice and virtue. In brief, Socrates is positive in his affirmation of these things, and he fears nothing apart from this loss of the soul and this view of the divine judge.

For this reason, he concludes that there is no struggle to which we should commit ourselves more keenly than that of ensuring that we can offer a perfectly pure soul to the Judge who looks upon everything. Whatever else men esteem is to be regarded with supreme contempt, and those things alone are to be honoured which are conducive to the eternal salvation of the soul.

Summary of the *Apology* of Socrates

THE ANCIENT theologians of the races of mankind are divided into three groups. Men in the first group merely sacrificed to daemons, for they lacked faith, I think, that the prayers of men would reach the beings in heaven. Men in the second group, however, worshipped the heavenly beings, believing that these possessed life and intelligence and that, by means of their rays, they looked around upon all things and heard all things, so that they graciously beheld the ceremonies of the sacrifices and hearkened to the praises and prayers of their suppliants. They believed, however, that the prayers of souls living in these bodies on earth were unable to reach those gods that have no dealings with physical bodies.

Men in the third group worshipped these gods above all others, deeming that whatever befalls the human race is fully embraced by the supreme causes through their consciousness and power. But they gave the name of gods to the visible bodies in the heavens as well as to the invisible super-celestial beings which our people call angels and which they themselves think of as the most intimate contemplators and ministers of the supreme God.

They considered, moreover, that providence is threefold. In God is universal providence, by means of which He provides and proffers all things to all beings. In the gods providence is not fully universal. By its means they give comfort to all by presenting them with gifts: not with all kinds of gifts, but with certain kinds. Finally, there is, in the daemons, a specific providence by means of which they bestow particular things upon particular people.

These theologians put the daemons into as many orders as there are stars in the sky, some being of Saturn, some of Jupiter, and so on. They locate all these orders accordingly: in fire, through their fiery principle; in pure air, through their pure airy principle; in gross air, through their gross airy principle; and in water, through their watery principle. They consider these watery daemons to preside individually over the individual kinds of living creatures and to be favourable to all life-forms endowed with sense-perception and quickening power.

Plato says that from the very beginning of evils these daemons have instilled desire into a great many creatures. He says that the airy daemons are more favourable to the rational power and that they separate it to some extent from the sensuous and quickening nature, while the fiery daemons turn the discursive power of reason to the contemplation of all that is lofty. And, as a result, the watery daemons rule over the pleasurable life; the airy daemons over the active life; and the fiery daemons over the contemplative life.

But since these people consider gods to be immortal and impassible, and men to be mortal and passible, they deem all daemons to be subject to passion, the higher and intermediate daemons being immortal, and the lowest daemons being long-lived. They say, moreover, that attraction towards the physical is in all the daemons. In the highest rank of daemons this attraction accords with the way of peaceful providence; in the second rank it is human but moderated; and in the third rank it moves down towards the agitations which we experience.

Again, they say that some daemons are natural, established as such from the outset, while others are wanderers, being men's souls put into airy bodies and men looking after those things to which they have grown accustomed. They also say that some daemons preside over more restricted areas and over cities; that some govern individual men, whose souls, falling into a body, have been allotted to a life according to their choice, becoming leaders and pioneers and judges of the life which has been chosen. In this way, some human souls come to conform to the nature of the Saturnian daemons, some to the nature of the Jovian daemons, and others to the natures of other stars.

The constitution of our bodies is distinct for a similar reason; and the animals, plants, minerals and stones likewise have different natures in accordance with the varied natures of the stars and of the daemons, with the result that some are solar and some are lunar, and so on.

The followers of Plato think that all the power of sacrifices, of oracles, and of divinations rests on what we have said. Indeed, following the earlier theologians, Plato himself and all of his own followers accept the account of the oracles as universally true, and they give reasons to support it. I merely refer to the fact that in the *Phaedrus* and the *Timaeus* he displays great faith in oracles. Indeed, in the *Phaedrus* he counts human wisdom as nothing when put beside words received from oracles and from states of divine frenzy; and in the *Timaeus* he says that the philosopher should proclaim only as much as is confirmed by divine oracles.

I leave out a great number of similar statements found in Plato's writings. In the *Apology*, of course, he takes prophetic oracles as the starting-point for the whole of Socrates' defence. In fact – and this is of the greatest import – he declares that the entire life of Socrates, the wisest and most just of men, has been established in accordance with the oracle of Apollo and the prophecy of his own daemon.

If you ask about the nature of Socrates' daemon, you will be told that it is fiery, because it raised him aloft to the contemplation of the divine. It is also Saturnian, because every day it wondrously withdrew the focus of his mind away from the body. It was also bestowed from the outset, rather than acquired, for he says that it came unto him when he was a child. It never incited, because it is not Martian, but it often restrained him from actions because it is Saturnian. Again, it did not give the spur to a man sufficiently inclined towards what is honourable, but it reined him back when it seemed that he might be deceived by fallacious conjecture when choosing a means to an end.

It penetrated his mind, bringing wonders to his eyes and sounds to his ears. But to which eyes and to which ears? Undoubtedly to the sight and hearing which pervade the whole ethereal body that underlies this manifest body. Now Socrates was able to perceive through the ethereal senses, withdrawing himself without difficulty away from the elemental senses. Whether sleeping or waking, he discerned wonders through those ethereal senses.

In a similar way, Avicenna shows that the prophets discern the form of angels and hear their voices. And why do Socrates and the few who are like him mention their own daemon? It is because few are daemonic by birth or training, while many are human, and most are brutes.

Again, why does he invoke his daemon at some times, and God at other times? It is because the lofty daemon, as the interpreter and messenger of God, inspired Socrates. But can we give the name of 'daemon' to the actual intellect of Socrates? Certainly we can. For Timaeus says that God has granted us the highest part of the soul as a daemon. Again, in the *Symposium*, the longing of the mind to contemplate divine beauty is called a daemon.

But apart from these considerations, it is necessary for a substance higher than us to rule over the daemons, for, as is shown in the *Symposium* and the *Laws*, the human race, being situated at a very great distance from the divine, needs some intermediate nature – the daemonic nature – to act as a conciliator. And it is not unjust that, as is shown in the *Statesman* and *Protagoras*, divine providence has set the nearer daemons over us like shepherds or, as he says in *Critias*, like helmsmen; for man, being placed in the darkness of ignorance and being racked by countless misfortunes or led astray by enticements, is unable to attain the end ordained for him by God unless he receive constant help from God. In this way he shows that God has entrusted us to the purer daemons as if to guides who would give help through prophecies, auguries, dreams, oracles, voices, sacrifices, and acts of inspiration.

Among these daemons he wishes us to understand that the friendly daemon of Socrates is different from the mind of Socrates. For his mind often motivates him, but his daemon never does. His mind is unable to teach without speaking or writing, but his daemon teaches many men through silence, as is shown in *Theages*. The fact that the daemon corrects Socrates with sounds and with signs indicates that it is beyond the mind. But if you are not happy to call a man's friendly guide by the name of daemon, then at least call it an angel, as people of our time like to do.

The *Apology* then obliges us to say something about oracles and statues. If you begin by asking why daemons do not perform nowadays the miracles that they were wont to perform, the answer is that Christ divested the evil daemons of their power and removed from men the entire worship of daemons as well as the daemonic art. If you next ask why the influences of daemons are drawn into statues or into men, listen carefully.

Every day something natural is drawn by art: a common example is wood which cannot be ignited by a small flame on account of its extreme density and which they coat with oil or immerse in sulphur and set ablaze with flames from kindling-wood. Every day, too, something divine is drawn by nature, when a delicate foetus in the womb, being disposed and shaped in a particular way, through nature draws a human soul from God, just as through magic a statue takes a daemon from the world. This is why the Egyptians, too, called nature great, finding magical power in the attraction of like for like, or, at least, of the harmonious for the harmonious.

Every day you manifest your voice, and every day you manifest the image of your countenance. But your voice and image are not always given back to you. A wall in a particular place returns your voice as an echo, and a reflective body returns your image to you. And so, be a mirror, be that wall, and you will immediately be within it, if I may put it in this way. For there you will be seen, you will be heard, you will be understood, just like the daemon in the statue.

125

If you consult Trismegistus, you will learn that a statue fashioned
with all due observances from natural materials of the world which
accord with a specific daemon is forthwith animated through that
concordant daemon. Trismegistus says that it is inspired either through
a daemon or through an angel, by which we may understand him to
mean a spirit that is less pure and a spirit that is more pure.

You will also hear this Hermes condemning many people of ancient
times because, not believing that there are divine powers above heaven
or that the prayers of people on earth rise to the higher heavenly
beings, they made statues as dwellings for the daemons, which they
worshipped as household gods. He clearly thought that, although
beneficent daemons were occasionally summoned into the temples,
harmful ones often came down.

You have heard in brief how daemons are drawn into the bodies of
statues. Now hear briefly how they are forcibly drawn into the bodies
of men. When the soul is wholly given over to phantasy through the
action of black bile or something similar, or through vice, it easily
becomes a dwelling-place for the lower daemons, whose presence
causes madness and gives affliction to both mind and body.

When the soul is turned wholly towards reason through the power
of philosophical purification, it becomes the home of the intermediate
daemons, from which it quite often receives the wondrous principles
of human life and occasionally the principles of natural life.

When the soul is wholly raised aloft to mind through the power of
devotion, it becomes a space open to receive the inspiration of the
highest daemons, the angels, by whose guidance it may wondrously
penetrate the mysteries of the divine world.

I see that you wish to understand which oracles Plato trusted most,
whether they were uttered by statues or by men. Know that he trusted
only those which were ascertained beyond peradventure to have come,
not through the deceitful daemons, but through the truth-speaking
daemons, the angels. For he had learnt from the mysteries of the
Egyptians that Jove had cast the impure daemons down to the lower
realms, that they might do their utmost to divert men, too, towards the
lowest regions; and from Pherecydes of Syros he had learnt that many
daemons had rebelled against Jove, their armies led by the snake-like
Ophioneus. He therefore deemed, most judiciously, that one had to be
on guard against such evil powers.

Socrates, for his part, being guided by his own particular principles,
entrusted himself to a certain oracle and to his own daemon, to be

directed at their bidding. Whatever the situation, in fact, he established his life in accordance with these two, with the result that he always put the eternal before the temporal; he feared injustice more than death; and in the service of truth, devotion, and love he would not hesitate to submit himself to toil, deprivation, contumely, insults, beatings, and death.

For him, truth engendered false calumny among others; love engendered hatred; devotion engendered blasphemous accusations and death. But he held all these things of little account, hoping to receive from the divine Judge good things for good.

Relying, therefore, on this hope and trust, he approached the judges without restraint and did not seek to acquit himself, but accused the judges themselves; and like a prophet declaring what was in store for those close to death, he proclaimed that after the wrong verdict penitence and punishment would ensue for them, while he went to the divine Judge, with wondrous joyfulness of mind and gladness of countenance.

I had decided to put an honourable end, at this point, to the theme, or, rather, to my little commentary, but two doubts are restraining me for a while.

The first is the well-known saying of Socrates, which has been repeated in this dialogue and frequently in others: 'The one thing I know is that I know nothing.' For here and elsewhere he states many things as if he has knowledge. But his saying is like another one: 'I said in my haste, All men are liars.' Thus Socrates is saying, 'Being withdrawn from the body, seized by a daemon, and enlightened by God, in the divine light I know one thing: that when I am united with the body I know nothing in the natural light. In the natural light, I say, I know not things as they are through the method of affirmation. For this kind of knowledge belongs to God, who embraces natures and their causes, since He Himself created them. Yet I know many things through a method of negation which, rather than saying what God is, states that He is not the body; which, rather than saying what the soul is, declares that it is not mortal; and which, rather than proclaiming what the absolute Good is, says that it is not this or that particular good.'

It is in this way that Socrates knows and teaches many things. And then there is the fact that his daemon does not incite him but restrains him: that is, the daemon gives him light to make negations rather than affirmations. But sometimes he does make affirmations, and great affirmations at that, such as his statement that he is filled with God rather than seized by the daemon. He is also affirmative when he adduces the evidence given by the holy men of old, or when he calls as witnesses the souls of men rising from the dead.

The second doubt is: Why does Socrates, who never doubts that the soul is immortal, use the disjunction 'Either no sense survives after death or some sense survives' at the end of the *Apology*? The first answer is that he is expressing doubt, not about every sense or every cogitation, but about our sense of what belongs to us, or something similar. This is what is meant by the words which are subsumed in the second part of the disjunction, where he says, as he does in the *Republic*, that abstracted souls know themselves in this way, both there and here.

At this point we should consider what is said against those who hold that souls transmigrate from body to body. Then we may safely reply that Socrates uses this disjunction at this time, not because he sees any need to doubt what he always holds to with unwavering conviction through the knowledge of negation as well as through divine inspiration and approval, but because he is now considering the persons of his adversaries, who, seeking in all ways to oppose him, are about to inflict death upon him as an undoubted evil.

Socrates therefore infers, to the contrary, that death is in no respect evil, whether our affairs are so or not, when he adds his apparently ambiguous statement about mortality for the benefit of those who, in the Epicurean manner of a sovereign, would have been able to mock Socrates as an easy prey to deception if he had denied that death was evil purely on the basis that after this life other good things continue to exist. Those eternal blessings, evident to Socrates but not to them, could not be proved in such a short space of time, but they are proved in *Phaedo* and in many other places.

But note the assured confidence of our Socrates, who, towards the end of the *Apology*, says to his friends, 'Be of good hope about death, for nothing evil can befall a good man, whether he be living or dead, as the affairs of a man who is in some way similar to God are not neglected by God.' To the judges, however, he exclaimed at the top of his voice, 'I, for my part, go from this place to die, you to live; which of us go for the better, God alone knows.'

Realise that he had no doubt about what he had just been affirming, but of himself and according to the method of affirmation he said that God alone knows, although a man may know this through God and through the method of negation.

Let us add that he dares not affirm that he is departing with a purified soul, but rather he affirms that the present journey will fully and immediately restore his soul to its celestial home.

Summary of *Crito*,
Dedicated to the Magnanimous
Lorenzo de' Medici

THE ARRANGEMENT of *Crito* is as orderly and as clear as that of the *Apology* and therefore requires no exposition. But take note first and foremost that, just as Socrates in the *Apology* uttered prophetic words in a wakeful state, so in *Crito* does he prophesy while in sleep, in order that you may know that God is always present, in wakefulness and in sleep, to the wise and holy man.

From all this, however, you should reflect upon his confirmation of the gospel teaching, his approval of the martyrs, his example of justice, his unparalleled courage, his scorn for the transient, and his yearning for the eternal: in short, the foundation of religion.

Need I remind you that the thoughts of the mob are to be spurned? That only the opinion of the wise, indeed of truth itself, is worthy of honour? That the choice we need to make is not to live, but to live well? That we must never do ill to our enemies or seek revenge for injuries received? That it is better to face the threat of death, and even suffer death itself, than to sin?

Need I mention his punctilious observance of the laws? Or his immeasurable love for his country? He unequivocally puts country before family and before life, for the very reason which he himself gives: that, departing to a new life, one must give the eternal Judge a fair account of the life just enacted and not be obliged to stand in fear of the laws which hold sway there, the sisters of the laws which obtain among men.

He concludes by declaring that the principles of kindly justice resound so clearly in his mind's ears that he cannot hear anything else; anyone who seeks to dissuade him will be making the attempt in vain.

He adds that there is only one way to follow, and that is the way which God, the divinely infused principle, reveals to us.

Summary of *Phaedo*

O UR BOOK on religion confirms something that is sufficiently well-known of itself: that the life of Christ is the ideal pattern of all virtue.

But the eighth book of our letters demonstrates that the life of Socrates is an image, or at least a reflection, of the Christian life. The Old Testament is confirmed through Plato, and the New Testament through Socrates. Anyone who doubts the validity of this comparison with Socrates should read Xenophon and Plato and the other writers who have drawn together the words and deeds of Socrates, and should attend particularly to Plato's *Gorgias*, *Apology*, *Crito*, and *Phaedo*.

Let us therefore proceed to run through the theme of this *Phaedo* at a brisk pace, or even in leaps and bounds; for we would seem to have given an adequate exposition of its mysteries in our *Theology*. Let us bear in mind one thing above all others: No one should be surprised that of all the reasonings pertaining to the immortality of the soul Socrates has here omitted that very one in which he places his trust in the *Phaedrus*, namely, that the soul is the beginning and principle of movement, from which it follows that the soul moves continually of itself and ever lives of itself alone.

Socrates has made this omission because this particular principle is common to our souls, to celestial souls, and to daemonic souls. In *Phaedo* the principles that need to be considered are those that relate more specifically to us.

But let us now look very briefly at the arrangement of the dialogue. The first thing to note is the wonderful way in which Socrates comforts his friends, who have actually come to greet and comfort him in prison, on the very day on which he is due to drink the poison. The second thing to note is the scrupulous devotion with which he heeds the premonitions even of his dreams, as if they were oracles, and the total care he takes to ensure that not even the slightest detail of the divine precepts is neglected. The third thing to be committed to memory is that men are under the careful protection of God and have no right to leave it unless God so wills. The fourth thing to note is what he earnestly wishes for himself when he says that he hopes on his departure to go to good men and to other good gods.

But he puts more emphasis on going to good gods than on going to good men; for when he first refers to other gods and to very good gods his understanding is that beyond the souls of the spheres there are the angelic minds, which are higher than the spheres and into whose company he hopes that our souls may one day be admitted; yet he dare not assert this because it seemed to many wise people that enough would be done for the soul if it were ever accepted into the company of the heavenly souls. Indeed, doubt is really cast over that part which he calls good men, for he does not then dare to affirm that the souls of men are good for the same reason that he called the gods good.

After this, when he is attempting to give comfort to himself and to his friends in the role of philosopher, he says: 'Since all the study of a philosopher is nothing but detachment from the body, and since he is brought closer to perfection every day by this detachment, he should certainly not fear the detachment from the body which occurs at death but should look forward to it with supreme hope and joy.'

Then he talks of two ways in which the philosopher detaches the soul from the body: firstly, he detaches it from agitation through the purifying work of moral training, and secondly, he detaches it from the senses and from the power of the imagination through the single-minded practice of contemplation.

Wise doctors make use of a double purging, firstly by softening and then by loosening, for they know that it will not be sufficient merely to soften and that it is unsafe to loosen before softening. Similarly, in the view of philosophers, moral purification comes first, like the softening process, for it does not root out the inward diseases of the imagination, the illusions. Then comes purification by self-examination, which sooner or later focuses its powers to disperse the misty exhalations of the imagination. But before the moral purification it is not safe to apply the operation of self-examination in case someone who is infected by vices were to misuse the single-mindedness of self-examination to defend injustice and impiety.

From this he draws the conclusion that the philosopher detaches his attention from physical things to the extent that he gives it to non-physical principles and Ideas.

But when he has enumerated all the inappropriate things which are imported into the soul from the body, he adds that the worst and greatest evil is that illusion by which the imagination very commonly distracts the mind which is lifting itself up towards the non-physical and diverts it to images of the physical and compels it to contemplate itself in some physical way.

Next, because the soul, when connected to the body, cannot pursue the truth of differentiated items which it naturally seeks, it infers the following disjunction: 'Either the truth is never pursued, or it is pursued after death.' That it is never pursued is not acceptable, for it is continually being sought by every soul.

Then he reproaches those who think that temperance is abstaining from the weaker desires of the body in order to fulfil the stronger ones. Again, he reproaches those who define courage as overcoming certain fears for the sake of those fears which have already overcome us. For his understanding is that every function of moral virtue is to be used to purify the soul for the sake of wisdom. If this were not the case, there would be no virtue.

Indeed, he calls human wisdom, too, some kind of purification, just as if he thought that by the meditation of our wisdom we pursue nothing but a kind of purity which is soon followed by divine illumination, and this is truly wisdom. His further meaning is that what unites us to God is not a state which has been acquired by our labours, but rather purification itself.

He then says that he will prove that the immortality of the soul is based on its forward and backward movement from one opposite to another. Just as the dead proceed from the living, so one day do the living rise again from the dead. Here he seems to foretell the resurrection of the dead, which he also acknowledges in the *Statesman*. In long, rambling excursions he further indicates that just as the substance of heaven, the material of the elements, unceasingly alternates between one disposition and another, so, too, does the rational soul – which is the origin of movement, life, and generation – have the power to endlessly alternate between uniting with the body and detaching itself from it, since many substances naturally change their qualities through perpetual alternation, and by the power of the soul an everlasting circuit is produced.

In what follows he finally asserts with unbounded confidence the resurrection which he has previously hinted at.

He then deals with the principle of remembering, having proved a little earlier that the soul lives prior to the body as well as after the body. But you should understand that such principles are Pythagorean. And from these you should choose what is most conducive to the truth. He says therefore: If learning is remembering, then souls have lived prior to the body. That learning is remembering he proves in two ways in particular.

Firstly, when we reply to someone who is asking questions in the proper fashion, we often speak the truth about things we have never learnt. Secondly, from the awareness of those things which are perceived we rise, through some unexpected abstraction, to the awareness of Ideas, just as, by recognising equals, we may rise to the appreciation of equality itself when we acknowledge that these things are different from those things, that they are striving to become similar, and that some things are more successful, others less so.

And since we do this throughout our life, we must have had the Idea prior to conception. For from the imperfect we did not suddenly receive the awareness of something perfect.

Now he shows in two ways that Ideas exist. Firstly, whatever object is called equal can become and can appear unequal as long as it remains the same in substance. Equality, however, can never become, or appear to be, inequality. Moreover, these equal things, being imperfect, partake of inequality, but equality itself can in no way do so.

In what follows, observe how strongly he affirms Ideas and how positively he adds that the essence of Ideas belongs to us. And observe that, since our soul relates individual things to Ideas, it is demonstrating that it is eternally at one with the essence of Ideas and is acknowledging this essence as its own. Observe also that in no circumstances is anything more important than taking the trouble to drive away the fear of death, as if it were the most serious illness, by giving proof of immortality.

Plato forthwith tackles another problem drawn from the relationship of the intellect to the intelligible. The intelligible itself he calls the incorporeal and everlasting Idea. And since the intellect is in harmony with it as its own object, he draws the conclusion that the intellect is also incorporeal and everlasting, especially as it rules over the body and is opposed to the transient.

But he confirms the relationship of the mind with Idea from the fact that whenever the mind is hindered it betakes itself to Idea and enjoys its fellowship and is made whole by it.

After saying that the soul is absolutely indissoluble, he added, 'or is close to something absolutely indissoluble.' You may understand this addition by referring to the *Timaeus*, where it is shown that God alone is absolutely indissoluble; but if other things are compared to God, they are considered dissoluble in some respect, because they are in some way composite; although those things which are composed in the best way, that is, in isolation from elemental matter, are never subject to dissolution.

Souls, therefore – our souls and divine souls – are close to indissoluble God. They are in some way dissoluble, but will never be dissolved. Furthermore, he gives the name 'absolutely indissoluble' to that in which neither essences nor any parts of action are distributed. The soul, therefore, although not distributed in accordance with the parts of essence, is yet dispersed through the parts of action, for it acts in time and by movement.

He adds, accordingly, that the pure soul goes after death to pure eternal realms, while the impure soul, being infected by things of earth, is pulled back to those things and often appears to be earthly. Indeed, when the attraction towards the physical remains in the soul, the result is not that the soul is actually seen – for attraction is not visible – but that the soul carries with it something that is visible: a kind of veil that is made of air or of the spirits and vapours of its own body, as Proclus says, or a veil new-woven from the circumambient air.

Plato is undoubtedly indicating here the same as Proclus: that between the ethereal body (which is immaterial, simple, and everlasting) and the earthly body (which is material, composite, and of short duration) there is the airy body, which is material, but in some way simple and of quite long duration, and in which souls continue to live even after death, until, when this has dissolved, they once more put on a composite body if they are not purified; but if they are purified, they go to heaven with their ethereal body alone.

The description of souls going into beasts is Pythagorean. It needs to be understood: our souls do not so much enliven the bodies of beasts as combine in some way, for the purpose of purification, with the imagination of brutes through their own brute imagination, just as people say that unclean daemons are often combined with the imagination of those who are mad. This is the explanation given by most of the followers of Plato, with the exception of Plotinus, who denies that the soul becomes a beast but says that it assumes, undergoes, or passes into the nature of a beast.

Plato draws the conclusion that only those are received into God who at death have been purified through the power of true philosophy. Listen: apart from the bond of the soul with the body there is nothing but love, which of its own nature gives provision. Again, whenever the soul acts through an instrument in relation to the forms that are subordinate to it, it really knows nothing, except when it turns of itself to the forms that simply exist within themselves.

Now learn, too, that from enjoying and feeding on physical things the soul becomes physical, and hence it is so completely deceived that it considers the physical alone to be true, although the exact opposite is the case. Such deception is the worst of all possible evils.

Furthermore, the soul that has already become physical falls after death to the realm of the physical, being a stranger to the non-physical. You may draw the conclusion that the soul which has been fully restored to its own purity does not entertain the slightest doubt about its own immortality.

The story of the swan is a Pythagorean allegory. It is Pythagorean because it says that the soul of the swan continues to exist; and the allegorical interpretation is that the swan is included in the category of solar creatures and that Socrates was solar because he won the approval of the oracle of Phoebus and also because he healed the minds of men.

Moreover, prophecy has four aspects – the divine, the daemonic, the human, and the natural – and this last aspect occurs in beasts through natural instinct. Understand, too, that swans are blameless men devoid of philosophy; they often have no fear of death and thus show that master philosophers should not have the least fear of death.

Next, note that it is extremely difficult in this life to understand the substance of the soul, for we see it in its physical manifestation; and thus the surest way to understand the soul is the way of moral purification and metaphysical abstraction. But when this is inadequate, we require some divine word or divine revelations and miracles.

We must now consider the mystery of the divine word as understood by Plato. He conveys two precepts in the discussion. The first is that we should not believe any principles without a lengthy weighing of the evidence. But once we have given our trust to any principle after due consideration, we must not readily abandon it in the light of any objections or analogies. The second precept is that in the discussion we should not consider our own person or that of anyone else, but we should consider only that principle which accords with truth.

There follow questions about the soul. Is it perhaps a blending of the humours? Does it exist prior to the body? Is it united with the body? Is it released from the body at some time? These questions Socrates answers in the following way.

If learning is remembering, then the soul existed prior to the body, and the soul cannot be a physical harmony. Indeed, since a harmony consists of its component parts, it does not precede them but is subsequent to them. If there is the same principle governing both harmony and the soul, then, just as one soul is not larger than another, so one soul will not be more harmonious than another, and therefore a temperate soul will not be a whit more harmonious than an intemperate soul. If harmony necessarily follows, and is led by, its component parts, then the soul cannot be a harmony of the body, which constantly leads in a direction opposed by the soul.

Moreover, before Plato fully resolves the doubts and fully deals with the principles of immortality, he speaks at length in condemnation of those who resort to assigning the causes of things to materials and instruments, and he asserts that the history of natural phenomena, in its entirety, is not adequately accounted for by natural phenomena themselves, for, in fact, all these things and their movements are utterly dependent on divine causes: the efficient, the final, and the ideal.

First of all, he chooses the final cause of each individual thing and of the whole, that is, the good of each individual thing and of the whole; and he says that the power of this good is the efficient cause. But since he is unable to embrace the full extent of the good, he then chooses the ideal principles of divine intelligence, the patterns in accordance with which all things are made manifest in the material nature of the world.

Note here how he confirms the Mosaic mystery, just as he does in the *Timaeus*: 'God saw that all things were good; indeed, that they were very good.' Thus all things are related to the Good itself.

Again, the soul which fixes its sight upon the physical is blind to the vision of the non-physical. The truth of things cannot be known unless we have recourse to Ideas. Besides, the patterns of the Ideas are within our minds, and it is in their conformity with these patterns that things are judged to be true or not. Socrates never broke his unwavering contemplation of Ideas, and his practice was to affirm Ideas alone. The undoubted cause of things is in Ideas, and the immortality of the soul receives its strongest proof from Ideas.

Forward movement among Ideas is from the least general to the most general, by way of those that are intermediate. Downward movement is from Ideas to their effects.

Finally, he bases the principle of immortality on the fact that the rational soul imparts life to the body, not as an accidental form inherent in the body but as a substantial form abiding within it and living on it in a particular form, like an Idea of physical life, and through itself effectively enlivening the body. For these reasons he draws the conclusion that the soul cannot undergo death, since death is opposed to life, while the soul has its own life and abides within itself and thus cannot undergo death either on its own account or on account of anything else.

Then, because the soul is immortal, he encourages everyone to undertake a training that is both moral and reflective, so that the soul, being purified and perfected through both the will and the understanding, may fly back to its heavenly homeland on these two wings. At the same time, he confirms that the soul is immortal because ultimately virtue imparts no harm, and vice imparts no benefit. But if the soul were not immortal, the hard life of virtue would harm good men, and the pleasurable life of vice would benefit evil men.

And in case someone should say that after this life vice is unable to harm or virtue to benefit, he adds that the soul carries with it its acquired tendencies, the habits, both good and evil, of the will and of the intelligence, to inflict immediate harm or bestow immediate benefit; for the truth is that a guardian spirit instantly takes all men to the divine Judge of life in the place appointed for the universal judgement, the less pure going to the air and the more pure to the ether; and there, being judged by another spirit, all men are drawn individually to their own kind along one of three ways: some to heaven, some to Tartarus, and some to the intermediate regions.

But a spirit guides them, stirring the understanding in good men but troubling the imagination and the emotions in evil men. And when he says that the wicked wander without a guide, he means without a beneficent guide. Moreover, they do not know whither they are being dragged, and they are seized violently.

Before he apportions the lots of the other souls, he describes the earth, saying that there are certain parts of the earth which are very extensive and so high that they are not buffeted by wind or storm. Here, under a most temperate sky, are produced things of the greatest value, and here are born long-lived men of the keenest sense.

There are those who would have it that the men and the other things generated here are compounded mostly of ether and air, with the least possible addition of the coarser elements, so that the bodies of the men are airy, being nourished by fruits which are as airy as possible. Lest anyone should deny this as an impossibility, Olympiodorus adduces the account given by Aristotle, who says that he saw a man who lived purely on air and sunshine.

He divides the form of the lofty earth into twelve regions because it accords with the twelve signs of the Zodiac, is ruled by the souls of the twelve spheres, and the twelfth is the sphere of the world; and, as the basis of everything, it has acquired for itself the dodecahedral shape which Timaeus attributes to the world. But in the *Timaeus* commentary we shall speak of this shape and of other questions pertaining to the earth.

Remember that living on this earth is like living in the earthly paradise described by Moses. He describes, in a similar way, the subterranean rivers by which souls are nourished. Everyone who explains these in accordance with the humours of our body and the disturbances of our soul which afflict us in this life adduces something akin to the truth, yet does not pursue the whole truth. For both here and in the *Republic* Plato indicates that the rewards for virtue and the punishments for vice relate most strongly to the next life.

Thus the subterranean river called Acheron is the place of purification and is related to cares and sorrows. It also corresponds to air and to the southern part of the world. Phlegethon corresponds to fire and the east: it has the power to punish through heat, and it punishes burning anger and lust. Styx and Cocytus correspond to earth and the west, and they punish hatred with mourning and weeping; the only difference between them is that Styx is described as flowing upwards and Cocytus as flowing forwards.

He says that Tartarus, the lowest of all, is the place of hell, in which the most profligate are afflicted by way of examples and not for the sake of being cured, as can be read both in this dialogue and in the *Republic*, as well as in *Gorgias*. Some writers add that Ocean, too, is in some way related to these rivers, and that it corresponds to water and the north; in it may be perceived the power to distinguish and define.

But understand that what is said of the rivers applies most strongly to the daemons and spirits which punish the wicked in the ways described. Of course, there are sins which are easily remedied, having not yet turned into habit. Those which are hard to remedy are the ones which have generated habit; yet they are committed with a certain revulsion in the reasoning faculty, and the people committing them show repentance. But the sins that are quite beyond remedy are those in which the habit keeps revulsion and repentance afar off.

Sins of the first type are purged in Acheron. Sins of the second type, if they incline towards the first, are punished in Phlegethon; and if they incline towards the third type, in Styx and Cocytus. The third type suffer affliction in Tartarus, from which, as Plato says, they never emerge. How this is explained by different writers I would rather leave out for the time being. Yet souls can be afflicted not only through the faculty of the imagination, which is wretchedly disturbed by the spirits, but also through the airy bodies which are called conveyances and skiffs.

Now Plato distinguishes the rewards in the following way. The souls which have lived just and holy lives without the aid of philosophy ascend to the lofty regions of the earth, such as we have described above, and dwell there in bodies that are very subtle and spirit-like. Those souls which have lived refined and philosophical lives dwell in heaven with bodies that are resplendent and celestial. But those souls which have been perfectly purified through the precise discipline of philosophy soar aloft to the super-celestial realm, where they dwell throughout the full extent of time without any bodies at all, as Plato says here.

On what principle some people explain this I choose not to recount. Porphyry and Iamblichus, of course, teach that souls which are wholly restored to God never fall. Conversely, souls in the opposite condition are deemed never to emerge from Tartarus. Whatever the case may be, countless revolutions are now undertaken, but it will be seen that the revolutions of time are employed for the sake of some purification.

Finally, Socrates declares that he owes a sacred cock to Aesculapius, and he requests that it be paid back most punctiliously. To Aesculapius the physician, son of Apollo, the ancients used to sacrifice a cock, the herald of the day and the sun. In this way they were declaring that they owed daylight – the light of life – to that divine beneficence which heals all ills and which is called the daughter of divine providence. In the same way he had previously wished to find a physician who would heal the ills of the soul.

And as if they were now completely freed from the disease of doubt and fear, he asks for thanks and a sacrifice to be returned to God. Moreover, the prophetic utterances of the ancients teach that the souls which go back to heaven sing paeans, or triumphal songs, to Phoebus. He therefore offers back to God the prayer that he may return to his celestial homeland singing gladsome songs of praise.

Summary of *Menexenus*,
Dedicated to the Magnanimous
Lorenzo de' Medici

P LATO'S AIM in *Menexenus* is to inspire in all men a supreme love
for their own country; and he achieves this aim in ways which dif-
fer from the methods he employs in *Crito*, the *Laws*, and the *Republic*.
In the present dialogue he achieves his objective in two particular ways:
firstly, by praising those who fearlessly face danger and death to protect
their country; and secondly, by extolling with the highest praise the
antiquity and virtues of his own country.

But take note from the outset that moral philosophy is absolutely
essential for a man who is going to govern a state; and that it is very
noble to die for one's country in battle, as is confirmed by the fact that
this action receives greater honour than all others in all nations.

Then observe the great harm wrought by flattery if an opportunity
is found for it in adulatory speeches. For in *Gorgias* he judges the
general level of oratory to be a type of flattery; in the *Phaedrus* he calls
the flatterer a beast that plagues the human race; and he attributes
something similar to the unclean daemon which continually
besmirches unwary souls with the filth of the body by using the bait of
harmful desire.

Moreover, in this present dialogue he considers the man who
flatters either privately or publicly to be almost indistinguishable from
a deceiver or a sorcerer, for such a man, being worse and more wicked
than a thief or a murderer, does not take from us our money or even
our physical life, but like a temple-robber seizes and carries off, under
the guise of a good action, that which is sacred: the discriminating
faculty of reason. Observe his power of deception; for with sublime
skill he practises his art of deception not only in matters that are
concealed but, wonder of wonders, in matters that are open to all.

For who does not clearly know his own ancestral and paternal
origin, as well as the size and shape of his own body? Yet even in these
matters we are encompassed about by poison-tongued flatterers who

140

exceed the cruelty of Circe in the harm they inflict upon men. For it is said that she changed the outward forms of men with her potions, but flatterers change a man's inner nature with their fawnings. Socrates accordingly mocks the rhetoricians because they fish for popular approval with all sorts of apparatus, and they praise others even more excessively than they themselves are praised, and they treat of a bagatelle with heavy concern and non-stop meditativeness.

He then develops a point he established at the outset: praise given to those who have died for their country encourages all men to defend their native land. For it was the ancient tradition of the Athenians to praise such men every year in the public assembly and to hold sacrifices in their honour.

But in case he seems to be giving undue weight to the power of oratory, he avers that he was taught this style of speech by a woman, Aspasia, for it was certainly not in Socrates' power to summon an assembly in the manner of the rhetoricians. He openly declares that such eulogies should be made, especially in funeral orations.

But he says that only in the Attic region were men initially brought forth from the earth of her own volition; while in other regions only brute forms were brought forth in this way from the earth. Take his words as you will: either as the words of a philosopher, or as the words of an orator. But you should be aware of Plato's view: after widespread floodings of the earth the land became so fertile from the sheer volume of water and from the heat consequent upon the floods that from her were born not only puny animals, such as we see today, but huge creatures and, in addition, human beings themselves.

He repeatedly confirms this point, both in this dialogue and in others. Numerous Egyptians held the same view, and many Greeks and Arabs eventually confirmed it, especially Algazales and Avicenna. Making use of this view put forward by the ancients, Aristotle says in his natural studies: 'Just as with small time-changes small creatures come forth from the earth, so larger creatures appear with larger time-changes, and with the greatest time-changes the largest and most complete forms appear.'

But wherever Plato draws forth living creatures from the very bowels of the earth, he appoints gods as the craftsmen and ministers of the master-builder of the world. By gods I mean the Ideas and type-principles inherent within the very life of the world and within the divine intelligence; through their agency, types of living beings are formed immediately after the floods as well as on a daily basis, whenever the physical seed for any such type appears to be lacking. In the *Theology* we have furnished adequate proof that this is what needs to happen.

But when man is born, not only does he stretch forth his hands as if to the other gods but he also appears as the mouthpiece and clear image of almighty God. Then he immediately sets the gods themselves over his children to be their guides and teachers; at least, this is what happened in earliest times.

You should, however, carefully select from all these things those which are more in harmony with the wisdom of Moses. Indeed, that which is most in harmony with Moses within this dialogue, as well as within *Protagoras*, the *Statesman*, and *Critias*, is the teaching that man was once brought forth from the earth, by the will of God, in the very likeness of God Himself.

But the kinds of floods that occurred, together with their times and causes, we shall recount in the *Timaeus* commentary.

Meanwhile, the man renowned for his piety will continue to honour his native land with awe-inspiring love and artistry, praising its origin, its form as a state, its everyday regulations, and its noble exploits, which in sundry places have been most highly extolled by other writers.

So let us bring our theme to a close with a few words that note such sentiments. All things are subject to power. Good fortune breeds envy, then ill-will, and finally dissensions and warfare. Everything gained immorally is worse than useless: it is harmful. Knowledge divorced from moral rectitude is not to be deemed wisdom but artfulness. Ancestral glory is dimmed in lacklustre scions who do not transmit the glory to their own offspring. Events must not be allowed to run of themselves. On all occasions one should live by the old adage, 'Nothing in excess'. The man who has so prepared himself that all things conducive to bliss hang upon his person, or the man who is very close to this condition, has established his life for the best. Be not raised up by joy or downcast by grief. Parents ought to consider that they have begotten children in order that these children might be good rather than immortal. Mournful wailings raised by members of the household grate upon the dead, if indeed they hear them at all. It is fitting to honour with solemn rituals those who have fought vigorously in battle to protect their country; their sons should be raised at public expense, and their parents should be cared for. To prevent the situation from becoming unbalanced, we should act with impartiality.

Summary of *Critias,*
or the Account of Atlantis

O UR PLATO, a most dutiful son of his native land, praised her in
Menexenus for her exertions against people of the East; and he
praises her again in *Critias* for her strenuous exertions against people of
the West. And in both dialogues he commends her for the numerous
gifts bestowed on her by God, by nature, and by art.

At the same time he warns us all not to be ungrateful to our native
land; and while he tells us that the power of Athens survives attack
from both East and West, he also teaches that everything is subdued by
power and that men endued with power conduct themselves rightly
and profitably both in Occidental (that is, adverse) situations and in
Oriental (that is, favourable) circumstances.

And after the *Timaeus*, which deals with the creation of the world,
Plato is quite right to wish *Critias* to be seen to deal with the antiquity
of the world. But he does not seem to have given any conclusion to this
account or to have written the subsequent account that was promised
under the title of *Hermocrates*. Yet he maintains that this account is true
and not fictitious.

In the first place, of course, whenever he imagines something,
his custom is to call it a fable; but here he does not hesitate to call it
history. In the second place, he takes the same stance in the *Timaeus*,
calling it amazing but totally true; and he mentions the two groups
who received the account with all due care: his ancestors and foreigners. For Critias received it from his grandfather of the same name, who
in turn received it from Solon, his paternal uncle, who committed it to
writing after receiving it from the Egyptian priests.

Moreover, Proclus adduces the accounts given by a certain
Marcellus concerning the deeds of the Ethiopians, in which these
things are unequivocally confirmed, being part of the Ethiopian
records. Although no follower of Plato denies the account, Porphyry
and Proclus, as well as Origen before them, consider that the literal

account contains an allegory. Lest these writers be ridiculed by Plato himself if they were to attempt to fit every detail precisely into an allegory, some well-considered allegories are given through the personage of a jesting Socrates at the beginning of the *Phaedrus*.

Indeed, lest we appear to be completely disregarding the anagogical meaning, which no true follower of Plato can disregard, Pallas should be seen as the goddess who presides over the intellectual life; Neptune, as the god who fosters and regulates generation; the Athenians, as symbols of those souls that are conjoined to bodies for the function of generation and the decorous provision of everything.

But it is very fitting that the substance and fluidity of generation indicate different things through the concepts of *West*, *Sea*, *Islands*, and various locations. Again, the war may be seen as the intense struggle through which the higher divinities strive to convert the lower ones into themselves and, with sword and fire, keep the souls away from matter and movement.

In the same way, when Neptune begot children from a woman, understand this to mean that he begot them from the earth, or that through some inspiration he reproduced new forms from previously existent life-forms. But his five offspring are the five physical forms which, with incessant movement, he compounds in this sea of matter: stones, minerals, plants, creatures devoid of reason, and creatures endowed with reason. Yet his children number ten, for at each birth twins are formed, since in every compound the elemental power takes root and there is a simultaneous infusion of the celestial power, which physicians call the special power. Thus from five twin-births there are reckoned to be ten children.

But the five zones or spheres which encircle the stronghold of Neptune are the natures of the five spheres: celestial, fiery, airy, watery, and earthy. When he says 'earthy in part' and 'watery in part', he is indicating both the stillness and the movement within things; and the general motion that pervades all things indicates the inter-active creative force within all things.

He also refers to minerals to help us to understand, through the seven minerals, the influences of the seven planets which affect the generation of all things. For the followers of Plato attribute gold to the Sun, silver to the Moon, lead to Saturn, electrum to Jupiter, iron and bronze to Mars, yellow copper to Venus, and tin to Mercury. Their measures and numbers are drawn partly from past records and partly from the principles of architecture, and to some extent they should be attributed to the grace and beauty of speech. But that is enough about allegory.

So let us now corroborate the mysteries of this book. The followers of Plato, if I may use their words, think that some gods are super-celestial, some celestial, and yet others sub-celestial. They call the first ones the children of God, and all the others they call the children of the gods. To the first they attribute providence in its widest sweep; to the second, providence that is less extensive; and to the third, providence that is restricted to relatively small matters. For they preside over delimited regions of the earth and over all kinds of created things according to the divine allocation, just as some celestial gods are placed over certain parts of heaven and over certain stars, while others are placed over others, and some sub-celestial gods have from the beginning undertaken to regulate certain nations, and others have the charge of other nations, according to a fixed scheme.

When I say 'from the beginning', I mean either from the creation of the world or from the beginning of the human race; for Plato holds that after the vast floods which swamped the earth men were divinely produced from Mother Earth as the creations of these gods. They were able to beget them, as if with a seed, through the Idea of 'human'; and the earth was able to bring forth, being saturated with moisture and being fertile from the increasing warmth: either warm sunshine followed floods or abundant rainfall followed great fires.

But the men begotten by the gods from the earth are called heroes, men who from the outset were guided for many ages by their parents through some mysterious persuasive power transferred from mind to mind. But since over a long period of time there was a gradual decrease in the divine power implanted in men's hearts and a corresponding decrease in the fertility of the earth, with the result that souls became devoid of all divinity and bodies became quite divested of their earlier fertility, God once again flooded the earth or consumed it with fire and restored our race to its primordial dignity through celestial movements so tempered by their mover that celestial fate always goes hand in hand with divine providence.

Indeed, just as physicians make their judgement about a human body, so do the followers of Plato make their judgement about the whole human race. For physicians say that life consists of the right quantity and type of some natural fluid and that it can be extended indefinitely, provided that the quantity and quality of the fluid is renewed, but not if the quality and quantity flowing in is less than that flowing out, as when someone daily fills a cup with wine from a great vat and straightway tops the vat up with water. For in this way the quantity of liquid in the vat remains constant, but the quality becomes less like itself every day, until finally, instead of pure wine, there emerges not merely watery wine but water pure and simple.

The followers of Plato believe that it is in this way that the divine and fertile quality previously imparted to the human mind by the gods and to the human body by heaven is gradually turned into human quality, which the human being naturally consumes until it degenerates into the quality of a beast. But such degeneration cannot be tolerated for ever by God, the disposer of all things.

But when Plato says, as he frequently does both in this dialogue and in others, that the gods had received diverse lots, you should understand that the gods are subject to that supreme One which apportions the lots; that the gods of necessity govern the region assigned to them; and that in divine beings necessity is profoundly voluntary, since among them there is a single will for the supreme Father and His children.

However, just as the elemental particles are conveyed to their respective places by that necessity which is going to be will for them, provided that they acknowledge it, so, for the gods, the very necessity of designated, natural, and executed government is identical with their will.

Moreover, when he says, in this dialogue as well as in the *Timaeus* and in *Menexenus*, that the Attic region was, above all others, fitting for men of great ability, you should remember that the followers of Plato disagree when it comes to giving reasons for this situation. For Panaetius thinks that the cause is the moderate warmth of the air: mid-way between great heat and severe coldness; and he proves that this is the case from Plato's own words in the fifth book of the *Laws* and in the *Epinomis*. Panaetius Longinus reasons that that region is often afflicted by extreme heat and extreme cold, and he says that the cause is the region's quality, which is a mixture of many things and is not patently obvious. Panaetius Longinus is reproved by Porphyry, who believes that the true cause of talent is physical.

Origen says in his commentaries on the *Timaeus* that it is caused by celestial aspects and influences; he bases his view on the eighth book of the *Republic*, where it is stated that certain celestial orbits are the causes of fertility and sterility for both the body and the soul. But Proclus says that in the same work Origen gave the true cause in part only, not having yet understood the whole of it. But Proclus himself, together with Porphyry, seeking the cause in something higher, says that the creative intellect of the world is the intellectual world and is, for that reason, apparently multiple; but the soul of the world, rather than being multiple, is the living, rational world; and it is very close to the universal space of the world, the space which is totally seamless and motionless, consisting of primeval matter and dimension; the space in which, prior to all those forms which are yet to be generated, the soul, from its own principles, which are consequent upon Ideas, impresses powers in different ways at different times, as if imprints of the mind-filled soul and individual receptacles were going to provide homes for various forms in various places and at various times.

Then different deities, having different regions allotted to them, illuminate and give form to their respective abodes. Thus the rational souls, having chosen their own elemental life, and chancing to be directed, by the revolution of the heavens, towards those regions in particular which are most suitable for the chosen form of living, directly fulfil the function of that life. And so, when they turn towards the life of Mars or Apollo, they at once obtain the region illuminated by Mars or Apollo and they fulfil the function of perfect courage or of prophecy. On the other hand, those souls which have chosen the philosophic life, the region inspired by the breath of Pallas, excel in both wisdom and magnanimity.

This is why Plato says, both in this dialogue and in the *Timaeus*, that the Attic region, being ruled by Pallas, accords well with wisdom and with military exploits. And in the fifth book of the *Laws* he says that the inspiration of local deities and local spirits is of the highest importance for the character and moral standards of the people. But he says that some moderation of the air is necessary, not as a cause but to prevent the work of the cause from being hindered.

For these reasons, the diversity of this place, according to the followers of Plato, does not create the diversity of character and ability, but rather supports and reveals it. For in this regard they think that there are three quite important factors relating to the elemental place: the disposition, natural or chosen, of the soul itself; the inspiration of local divinities; and the celestial influences.

But hindrances can come from a commingling of the elements, from an unusual conjunction of planets, or from any calamity that may befall the human race; and those good things which are poured down from above are rendered bad by the obstruction of the lower world.

This is a matter we have discussed in the *Laws*. But enough on this subject for now.

From all the mysteries of this book you may simply gather that the freedom of the human will runs hand in hand with Providence. You should also gather a belief similar to the one expressed by Moses: that men once lived blessed lives in a paradise of delights, as they say, for as long as their innate grace and justice flourished within them. But when that grace vanished through intemperance and pride, they fell into abominations and grievous adversities. Yet God washed away the sins of men with a flood of waters.

Whatever may be missing from this account can be quickly made good from the beginning of the *Timaeus*. This is an account of events occurring before the Flood. The man who was going to speak of what happened after the Flood was, I believe, Hermocrates. Those nine thousand years will not cause you any concern if you listen to Eudoxus, who says that the Egyptian years were not solar but lunar. *ie months*

The final part of this book teaches that Jupiter, or God, the master-builder of the world, looks from his throne (that is, from his own self-awareness) upon all things far removed and most minute and turns all the deities under his command towards that same throne (that is, towards contemplation of the divine); and being thereby prepared, these deities govern what is below them. On the other hand, they do not actually do these things, for it is simply by contemplating the divine that they regulate the temporal by means of the divine.

This seat he calls the central throne of the world because from it as the centre all things flow forth, and to it they all flow back, and from it all things are readily descried and contemplated.

[Left margin handwritten notes:] Addresses problem of title 'Timaeus substantiate for SS

Time spent from Adam to X being too short.

PART TWO

Discussions of
the Twelve 'Letters of Plato'

piter didn't create world in Plato, Demiurge did

remeatio

Translator's Notes to Part Two

1. The word which Ficino uses to name his discussion of a letter is 'argumentum', a word which suggests the theme or subject of a document.

2. The first letter is written by Dion, who, according to Ficino, 'not only heeded Plato's words but also put them into practice'.

3. Of the fifth letter, Ficino says that, although tradition ascribes it to Plato, 'it seems, in fact, to be from Dion, who is using all his powers to fashion Plato, in all respects, within himself.'

4. As with Part One, it is not the translator's intention to consider questions of authenticity, spuriousness, and dubiousness, but to present what Ficino says.

Discussion of the First Letter,
Written by Dion

DION OF SYRACUSE, an undoubtedly great man, who not only heeded Plato's words but also put them into practice, immediately and open-heartedly gave back to the tyrant who banished him the money which the tyrant had previously sent him; and as a true follower of Plato he gave Dionysius the greatest blessing in return for the greatest wrong, by offering him three wholesome precepts.

The first of these precepts is that princes perish not from lack of funds but from lack of friends. The second is that there is no power greater than the unanimous support of good and prudent men. The third is that we should acknowledge the wrongs we have committed and see to it that, in view of the harm our wrong-doings have inflicted upon us, we shrink from any future transgressions.

✻

Discussion by Marsilio of the Second Letter, which Plato wrote to Dionysius, *But as ed* Tyrant of Syracuse

+ transl. says . it seems to be authored by him

I N THIS LETTER, which he writes to Dionysius the Younger after
his first banishment by him, and after the expulsion of Dion, Plato
says that there are four things to be observed above all others.

The first is that great power and wisdom seek one another through
some natural impulse, so that they may come together in union. This
is what we have found in the divine world, in nature, and in art.

Firstly, within the Godhead, God's boundless wisdom accompanies
His limitless power. This is what he indicates by the names of Jupiter
and Prometheus. He says that Jupiter is power, while Prometheus is
providence. He considers power to be the fount of divine intelligence,
and also its mirror; for we understand through the power to understand, and in understanding something we look upon its power.

Their marks are found in nature, too, for in those things which are
compounds by nature – stones and minerals, plants and animals, and
even the first things in the heavens – the natural composition is such
that from the inward power of nature and from natural forces there
arises a particular order within the forms of these things and within
their actions and effects. But this order, manifesting outwardly and
accompanying the inward force of power, is seen to reveal a degree of
wisdom. For in its regulated movements nature's way is not different
from that of wisdom, but their ways are identical in all respects.

In human art, too, both private and public, a similar harmony of
power and wisdom is apparent. The natural capability of talent,
memory, and will pertains to power. Once power has been acquired,
wisdom arises from it, and the very order which pertains to wisdom is
preserved in actions. *true*

Of this mystery, which works through the divine world, nature, and
art, we have examples in the fine custom which Plato mentions: the
mutual friendship and, as it were, natural intimacy between the

a stupid but Ficinian arg. by analogy w stars

powerful and the wise. On this matter he directs us to the heavens, in which the planets that indicate princes are closest to those that indicate the wise. For Jupiter is closest to Saturn, and the Sun hardly departs from Mercury. According to Plato, the rule of conduct arising from this is that princes should honour the wise, and the wise should freely counsel princes. For wisdom without power benefits few, and power divorced from wisdom is injurious to many. *aphorism*

Howard Dean

Geo. Bush

Indeed, the greater the power, the more injurious it is when devoid of wisdom. And wisdom remote from power seems defective. This is shown by the great conjunctions of the planets, for Jupiter is the lord, and Saturn is the philosopher, but nothing great or lasting is wrought by them except they be in conjunction with each other.

Plato's meaning is that happy friendship arises between the powerful and the wise, while the happiest union of all occurs when power and wisdom are conjoined within a single soul. In such a soul resides the divinity of Pallas, uniting power with wisdom; for Pallas alone excels in the arts and brandishes her spear at the same time.

So far we have spoken of the first mystery of this letter. Let us now move on to the second mystery. *first time he bragged called it*

The operation of the soul which is raised up by goodness is to enjoy the Good which is fully divine and knows no limits. It is this which *that* benefits most people for the greatest length of time. Such is the true glory of virtue, bestowing learning and good practices upon present and future generations.

Men, therefore, who are endowed with the best characteristics rejoice for two reasons in particular: because they love the light of virtue which shines in their heart, they also cherish the outer splendour of virtue; and because their constant wish is to benefit as many people as possible through this splendour, they rejoice in this continual benefit conferred upon the human race. *Sounds like fame?*

They rejoice, I say, as far as their perception extends; but since they strive to benefit posterity with unending glory, in the hope that they will rejoice then, as now, in this splendour and benefit, they predict that they will perceive it plainly once this life is over, for they are urged towards this immense benefit by the impulse of a more divine nature, not because they rejoice in it now but rather in order that they may rejoice in it. And if many types of creature, in the care they give, at nature's prompting, to their homes and food, do not look in vain to future use and enjoyment, much less will the outcome disappoint those divine souls who hope to enjoy some everlasting benefit. *pie in the*

sky by and by.

The prophet Daniel understands the splendour and benefit of such virtue, both in his teaching and in his life, for he says: 'And they that be wise shall shine as the brightness of the firmament; and they that turn many to righteousness as the stars for ever and ever.'

But in some souls that decline from their own divinity the benefit which is the zeal of true glory is either extinguished or transformed into vainglory.

The third mystery of this letter reaches greater heights; but since we have expatiated upon it in the *Theology* and in the book *On Love*, it will be enough to give just a taste of it here. When we consider carefully the forms that are made by the craftsman, we gradually realise the principle on which they have been made; and when we apprehend the principles by which the craftsman makes the forms, these principles grant us easy access to the Ideas of the creative mind: those Ideas in accordance with whose patterns he has directed his own principles in order to produce the forms.

But just as, with man-made objects, we can proceed from forms to principles and can move from these principles to Ideas or models, so, in contemplating the natural order of things, we can acknowledge that the most beautiful forms of things are constructed on the most artistic principles; and if on principles, then on Ideas or models, according to whose likeness principle itself produces forms from its own level.

Thus there are three levels in the universe: that of forms, that of principles, and that of Ideas.

Now the level of forms, which are perceptible to the senses, is referred to the soul of the world, that soul which, as the beginning of movement, begets forms within matter, but begets different forms through different principles and seeds. We refer this level of principles within the soul to the mind, which is higher than the soul, that mind from whose Ideas the soul receives the principles for governing all things. Lastly, the level of Ideas comes down into the mind from the limitless and undivided glory of the divine Good, since the single Idea of good men, which is God Himself, infuses the angelic mind with the varied Ideas of varied good things.

For this reason, the three levels of things are related to three primary origins: the level of forms is related to the world-soul; the level of principles, to the angelic mind; and the level of Ideas, to the Good Itself.

And because all things are related to the Good through Ideas, Plato says, 'Around the King of All are all things', meaning that around the

the metaphysics here is difficult. I'm not sure whether this is Plato's, Ficino's, or the translator's fault. It is particularly helpful to have the metaphysics translated

Good Itself are Ideas and, through Ideas, all things. Around the second, or the mind, are the secondary items, the principles which follow the Ideas. Around the third are the tertiary items, that is, around the world-soul are the forms.

But when he says 'around', he means that God is the model cause of things. When he says 'by His grace', he means that God is the final cause; and when he adds 'He is the cause of everything beautiful', he means that God is the efficient cause, for the fact that some things are deformed is due not to what they receive from Him but to the extent to which they fall away from Him.

yes, not ok

So

And it is not surprising that the followers of Plato wish it to be seen that Plato named each of those three primaries, for the names he gave them were similar but not identical. God, in fact, exists through Himself and the one Good. But since unity and goodness are limitless, it follows that God *is* through Himself absolutely. The supreme mind, being closest to God, *is* through God, inasmuch as it is something unitary and good, and also through itself, inasmuch as it is mind and at the level of the second nature. Lastly, the world-soul arises from the primal God, insofar as it is unitary and good; from mind, insofar as it is mind; and from itself, insofar as it is subject to movement.

ie, angelic?
?
?
?
d if the ven tia ties
n—s.

This is the limit to which Plato says that the origins of things divine and the principles of all other things extend.

So nothing up to now

Moreover, he declares our soul to be divine when he adds that it strives after things divine but does not grasp them as long as it gazes upon those things which are related to it: the senses and whatever the senses perceive, or the forms conceived by the soul through encountering those things. For all these things are very different from things divine; and so the soul, gazing upon them, is obliged to feel and speak about divine matters as other than they are.

has referred to man

There follows the fourth mystery, concerning the perception of things divine. Initially, he says that the pursuit of the divine, not being carried out correctly, that is, not being organised according to the due steps of purification and discipline, is the cause of all evils, because those who pursue God wrongly eventually reach a point where they either deny the existence of God or state things about God which are not of God. This is how true religion perishes, and once religion has perished the flood-gates are open to all evils.

4

Secondly, he says that the impulse to pursue divine matters is the cause of evils; that is, if we misuse this impulse and use it in any way we wish, it obstructs the enjoyment of present delights and calms those

!
Well ...?

purification and discipline prevent theological error!

155

calms those who, in this life, are panting for higher things. But what does he mean when he says 'Unless a man remove this impulse from his soul, he will never attain the truth'? He certainly says that the truth of things dependent on God cannot be had unless the truth about God be held first.

Moreover, through the words that he adds next you can understand that Plato himself often took great pains to pursue matters divine; and those who first heard Plato reflecting on the divine were instantly blinded by the overpowering brightness of the divine, and they were troubled for a long time, until they were finally able to separate the mind from the dispositions of the senses and from the projections of the imagination; and when this had happened through some divine dispensation or divine light, they began to discover the truth, which until then had been hidden.

It was for these reasons that Pythagoras, whom our Plato honoured in all matters, always began the holy mysteries of his teaching with the most scrupulous purification of the mind, and he always taught, just as Plato teaches, that those mysteries should not be divulged to the public, who, taking them amiss, would despise them or fall into error. For if you announce to the public that God has within Himself none of those things which are perceived through the senses, either they will laugh at you or they will say that there is no God.

Hence the words of Lysis, the follower of Pythagoras, to Hipparchus: 'It is not right to share the mysteries of philosophy with those who cannot even dream of the purification of the soul.'

There are, moreover, some mysteries of the theologians concerning God which would trouble not only the general public but also many cultured people. One of these mysteries is that nothing intelligible should be affirmed absolutely about God; for whatever is delimited by intelligence is bound to fall short of a God who transcends all limits.

Thus many erudite people are not ready for these deeper mysteries, just as the general public are not ready for less profound ones. The situation is such that although some people are equipped with shrewdness of intellect, a strong memory, and clear judgement, and although they have heard these things for a long time, they do not fully understand them; for even if they are born for other things, they are not born for matters theological; or if they are born for such matters, yet they are not adequately instructed and trained for them; and if they are so instructed and trained, then they have not been screened from inner agitations by the benefit of more mature years.

156

Now because agitation causes movements and distractions in various directions, and leads towards matter, it renders the mind a stranger to God, than whom nothing can be conceived that is further away from movement, from diversity, and from matter. Lysis was therefore justified in giving his warning to Hipparchus.

read Lis [margin annotation]

It is worth considering how much time we spent removing the stains imprinted on our hearts, before we were worthy and able to hear the precepts of Pythagoras. Moreover, anyone who betakes himself to God with a calm and well-instructed intellect will be quite deceived about God by his own intelligence, just as the general public are deceived by their senses and imagination, and just as many educated people are driven away by their own agitations. For intelligence, when judging according to its own nature, compels us to assert that God Himself is either an intellect of some kind or something intelligible.

But the limitless Good is not the intellect, which turns like a beggar towards the intelligible as towards something good from whose illumination it may gain some advantage; and it should not be described as the intelligible, which has a nature shared by the intellect, a nature through which it also has some similarity with intelligence. But there is no relationship or similarity between the limitless Good and the limited good things of nature.

Thus he shows in *Parmenides* that we have no name for God, no definition of God, and no knowledge of God, for He is beyond all the bounds of our understanding.

Prior to Plato, Hermes makes the same assertion; and subsequently to Plato, Dionysius the Areopagite does the same, showing that God cannot be described as an intelligible being, but is above both 'being' and 'intelligible'.

For this reason, since God infinitely transcends the intellect and the intelligible, no one can attain the divine substance by any action of the intelligence, but this substance can eventually be attained by devotion, I mean a propitious devotion, through the gracious work of the limitless Good that has been conveyed to us, conveyed, I say, into unity itself as the head of our mind, when the mind gathers itself wholly together from all directions into its own unity, which is the express image of divine simplicity. But because, under the divine Sun, it glimmers for the mind which is clothed with this unity, it completely departs when unity is removed and multiplicity is donned.

From all this it is quite clear that, in the view of our Plato, the divine cannot be discovered by us but is revealed to us from above; that the substance and nature of the divine cannot be understood by the mind or explained in words or writings. These things should therefore be discussed and described with the hope that we may give encouragement through our words and writings and prepare souls for things divine, rather than offer proof.

This is why Plato writes nothing about the definition of the divine substance and the divine nature. He does, however, write a great deal which, through negations and narratives, exhortation and instruction, will one day lead to that state of mind to which the halls of almighty Olympus will open their gates.

When the mind has withdrawn itself to itself and away from all that is lower, and when it turns from itself to all that is higher, it immediately attains, at a single stroke, unity and steadfastness and simplicity, if I may express it thus. But what it attains, according to St Paul, it is unlawful for men to utter and, according to Plato, much more unlawful for men to write, lest what is holy be given to the dogs.

Yet although he trusts neither words nor writings with the explanation of matters divine, he considers it safer to entrust it to words than to writings, for writings become the property of all and sundry. However, he allows such words to be spoken to only the most carefully chosen people. But he judges that in all respects the worthiness of things divine requires us to communicate in words from mind to mind rather than by writing upon external materials.

For this reason, the Jews say that the mystical meaning of their Law was not communicated in writing by God Himself through Moses, but was rather entrusted to their souls. This is what they understood.

The followers of Pythagoras certainly observed this practice, and so did Plato. For even here he promises to send some things through Archedemus rather than in writing. But he declares that what he has written are the words of Socrates, whose real function was to purify.

But why does he add that Socrates, even in his youth, was beautiful, that is, enlightened by God? It is so that we may understand that Socrates, through the completion of his early education and through his own propitious nature, was quick to receive from God, through his personal daemon, those things which other people have difficulty in attaining even after long and arduous toil. It is also that we may understand that those mysteries which had been received through divine revelation had been communicated to Plato and can also be communicated, through Plato's counsels, to men of like disposition.

But in case someone is thinking that I have gone into a dream during this exposition, it is important to hear Proclus' confirmation of these things: 'For those who desire to attain the Highest Good, what is needed is not knowledge or the exercising of talent, but steadfastness, rest, and tranquillity. Indeed, it is divine faith which draws us and unites us ineffably to the Highest Good and to all that is divine. It is certainly not through knowledge or any action performed by our own wits that we should seek or aspire to the Highest Good, but we should offer and commit ourselves to the divine light and, with our senses stopped, we should come to rest in that unknown, hidden unity of all beings. For this kind of faith is more ancient than any teaching.'

It is clear that this is what Proclus has received from Plotinus. But anyone who considers these things carefully will not require of Plato the pattern of teaching which he usually adopts with the human disputants in his dialogues, but will be content simply with that style which takes a more direct route to God.

But such a style or arrangement consists in purifying and re-directing; for the mind's eye needs to be purified of the dark squalor of matter and, when cleansed, it needs to be rightly directed towards the light of the divine Sun. But it is not necessary to seek or to strive beyond this; for the boundless light, present everywhere through its own nature, floods the eye of the mind as soon as this eye, fashioned in its likeness, looks back to it in purity.

And if the intellect, in order to look up to God, earnestly applies its own inherent activity, which is something non-essential and multiple and, in its own way, subject to movement, it will certainly be separated in some way, through this activity, from the perfectly single substance of God and from all reflections of movement, however remote. It will therefore be sufficient, after appropriate examination, to have purified and re-directed the mind.

Hermes attributes all else to the sacred silence of the mind; for God, he believes, is known to the mind by His silence rather than by His words. This is why the dialogues of Plato focus on this point: some on purification alone, some on turning alone, and some on both. But these mysteries are re-affirmed in the letter to the Syracusans, and, being confirmed, wonderfully confirm in their turn the teachings of the Gospels.

Discussion by Marsilio of the Third Letter,
Written by Plato to the Tyrant Dionysius

T HIS LETTER from Plato is written to Dionysius the Younger,
after Plato's second banishment by him. He first answers some
questions from Dionysius; then he rejects the charge levelled at him by
Dionysius.

Thus, in answering a question, he teaches that within God there is
none of that pleasure which has pain as its opposite and which consists
in movement and in the satisfaction of some want. But he does not
deny that within God there resides the whole of that good whose cause
appears as good delight. He adds that the pleasure that is changeable is
the cause of harm with regard to gains and honours and of pain with
regard to the body; and that such pleasure destroys keenness of mind,
memory, the power of judgement, and dignity.

Then, in answer to the charge made by Dionysius, Plato proves that,
having set off for Sicily for the most just of reasons, he openly gave
counsel on the restoration of previously derelict cities and on impartial
government.

Discussion by Marsilio of the Fourth Letter,
Written by Plato to Dion of Syracuse

AFTER DIONYSIUS has been driven from his tyrannical position, Plato writes to Dion, who has now returned to his homeland, giving counsel to him and to Heraclides and Theodotus and other friends who held power in the state, that they should live as strangers to tyranny and hold to government by the aristocracy, moderated to some extent by the views of the people.

Here are some precepts to commit to memory: firstly, it is the duty of the leaders to excel all others in truth, justice, magnanimity, and temperance, and in all respects to excel all others in prudence as much as men excel boys in prudence; secondly, they should conduct themselves as they wish to be seen; thirdly, they should bear in mind that the eyes of all are turned upon them, and thus they would remember that their vices cannot be concealed and that they will not satisfy expectations with a virtue that is no more than average; fourthly, they should imitate the most upright lawgivers and avoid like the plague disharmony with their fellows; fifthly, they should remember that the common good is crucial in the conduct of their affairs, and that this can be obtained and preserved purely by the cultivation of the inner man.

Seems contradictory. Similarly P. previously says (acc. Fic, cf that the way to benefit the most people is to contemplate the idea of the Good.

Discussion of the Fifth Letter

A LTHOUGH TRADITION ascribes this fifth letter to Plato, it seems, in fact, to be from Dion, who is using all his powers to fashion Plato, in all respects, within himself.

The letter instructs Perdiccas, a leader established in a monarchy, to remember that he is a young man and thus stands in need of the counsel and service of older men: not of all older men, but of the most upright of them, and not in every matter, but in matters of ruling, for they understand the most fitting way to rule, whether it be rule by one, by a few, or by many.

The voice of government is its spirit and life, the law, which must establish and accomplish appropriate duties towards God and man. If it does not, it cannot survive.

But since Dion indicates that he and Euphreus, being filled with the teaching of Plato, are holding to those things which pertain to good civil order, and to prevent Perdiccas from despairing of this matter, especially since Plato himself never benefited his own people with citizenship training, he adds that Plato recognised that his people were suffering from an incurable disease, and for that reason, following the practice of prudent physicians, he had no wish to undertake, in vain and to his own peril, the healing of an incurable animal.

Discussion by Marsilio of the Sixth Letter, Written to Hermias, Erastus, and Coriscus

THE DIVINE Plato exhorts Hermias, Erastus, and Coriscus, princes of lands with common borders, to live in true harmony, prophesying that they will find safety solely in such harmony, by means of which, with the blessing of God, who delights in unity, they will acquire all good things and eventually reach that state in which, once all their affairs are properly settled, they will have the strength, as is only right, to pursue with whetted zeal that wisdom which is divine rather than human.

He states that lasting harmony can be established among them only by agreement that is lawful and is ratified by common consent through properly performed sacred ceremonies and through the taking of an oath, calling upon God Himself as their witness and praying to Him as the author and preserver of all unity: calling upon God and praying to Him, I say, with the uneven number in which, it is said, God delights. For in this letter Plato adduces the three principles of creation which he also touched upon in his first letter.

When he refers to the leader of all things present and future, he intends us to understand the soul of the world, which, being the principle of movement, uses the process of time to bring all things into the present from the future and to take all things from the present into the past. When he speaks of father and lord, he means almighty God and the Good itself. But midway between these two he seems to place a divine mind, because when he repeats 'of the leader' he adds 'and of the cause'.

For in the writings of Plato, 'the king' often stands for the Good itself, 'the cause' stands for the mind, and 'the leader' stands for the soul. And since Plato relates the cause to the mind, his followers reason in the *Timaeus* that the intellect is the child of the Good itself and the craftsman of the world. On this point there are the words in *Epinomis*: 'Reason most divine, or the most divine Word, decked the visible world'.

But here he calls the Good itself 'father' or 'lord', indicating by the first name the father of the mind, and by the second name the lord of the soul. This is perhaps the explanation that Platonic number will give, and likewise a Christian follower of Plato, albeit an Arian.

Perhaps, too, there will be someone who will be able to understand 'leader' as the Holy Spirit, and 'mind' as the Son. For when Plato says 'father', he includes the Son. And anyone who posits a single essence of the three will seem to fly in the face of many followers of Plato, but will not openly oppose them.

Now Plato encourages the weightier pursuits of learning together with the more delightful but related pursuits of fine speech, poetry, and music. He bids all men devote themselves to these pursuits, hunting out the divine fragrance through such clues, that they may come to love the divine fragrance alone and thus pursue the divine taste even further. He therefore says that if we consider God truly, or consider Him in this way – that is, if we pursue Him by loving Him, or love Him by pursuing Him – we shall all, beyond peradventure, eventually come to know Him.

Indeed, the name 'philosophy', although seeming to convey some sense of searching, in fact conveys love and a loving embrace. Thus Pythagoras recognised, as did Plato, that we have one relationship with good things which are finite, and a different relationship with the infinite Good: finite good things are known by us before they are loved, and when they are known they are thought worthy of being loved; but the infinite Good is loved before it is known, and is thought worthy of being pursued not because it is known but rather because it is loved. But why is it lovable before it is understood? This is because love, conveying the lover into the beloved, supplies what was lacking in the relationship and effects the transformation through desire.

In the scriptures, is not God often described as fire? By a similar metaphor, then, an angel is described as a transparent body, and the soul as an opaque body, that is, as long as the soul is enclosed in this dark dungeon. And so, just as, near fire, a diaphanous or transparent body, being like air or water, at once admits light from without and from within, while earthy bodies need to be vigorously heated and refined by the heat into the likeness of a diaphanous body before they can assume the fiery light, in the same way the spirits which are separate from the body receive the divine light immediately, while the spirits which are conjoined to earthy bodies require the fire of trans-forming love. When they are purified by this love and changed into the divine likeness, they finally shine all around with the divine splendour of knowledge.

This is why Porphyry says: 'The inquiry into matters divine purifies the soul, but love deifies the soul.' For he truly expresses the situation with these words, and he is quite right to do so, since no material turns into fire from receiving light but from receiving fiery heat.

Hence the view of Plato is that we should pursue divine things, by which he means the things which are, and also such things as are objects of general observation, but that at the same time we should love them, not with a general love but with a singular and incomparable love; for in this way alone shall we be blessedly happy.

Only a profane man fails to understand the degree to which these words accord with holy writ. *I won't project again.*

Discussion by Marsilio of the Seventh Letter

T HE SEVENTH LETTER of Plato was written to Dion's relatives and friends, after the country was given its freedom through the work of Dion and after Dion was unjustly put to death.

But in order that many things relating to history, both in this letter and in others, may be clearly understood, it is necessary to go over them a little more thoroughly.

Plato travelled three times to Syracuse: once at the age of forty, in the days of Dionysius the Elder; and twice later, when Dionysius the Younger ruled as the tyrant. But what he did on each of these journeys, or why he made them, can be found partly in the biography which we wrote of him and partly in these letters.

Now Dion seems to have been of the same family as Dionysius and to have had various other connections with him, since Dionysius had previously married Dion's sister, Aristomache, while Dion had married Dionysius' daughter, Areta. But Dionysius the Younger was not the son of Dion's sister but was the son of another wife, named Doras.

During Plato's first visit, Dion became one of Plato's 'hearers' and thus directed his life towards virtue and began to strive for the common weal of his country. And so, on the death of Dionysius the Elder, when Dionysius the Younger became the tyrant and, being still a child, was to be ruled in all respects by Dion's counsel, Dion chose to direct him towards a desire for the philosophic life and summoned Plato to Syracuse with many entreaties and also persuaded Dionysius to invite him.

Plato therefore complied, being drawn initially by the hope that through his counsel he would bring it about that the government would change from a tyranny to a republic or a monarchy. But about four months after Plato's arrival Dionysius, persuaded by false accusations, banished Dion as a conspirator against his tyranny. In spite of that, Dionysius was happy to embrace Plato. But Plato, displeased with the failure of his mission, returned to his own country.

166

He made the third journey with the aim of reconciling Dion and Dionysius, having been repeatedly entreated by both of them and having also been solicited by Archytas and Archedemus, as well as by very many noble followers of Pythagoras. Then Dionysius promised to recall Dion and to adopt the best form of government. Yet he did not keep either of these promises.

But when Plato openly withstood Dionysius because he had broken both his promise to him about recalling Dion and his promise to Theodotus about keeping Heraclides unharmed, he enraged Dionysius. And so Plato now lived in imminent danger of being killed by the soldiers. But Archytas of Tarentum sent the orator Salmiscus to Dionysius with a ship, asking him to send Plato away. Dionysius sent him away and gave him free passage. Plato returned to his own country safe and sound.

Shortly afterwards, Dion secretly raised an army, marched on Syracuse, drove out Dionysius, and gave the Syracusans their liberty once more. Dion, himself, however, was killed shortly afterwards through the evil intent and envy of his own men.

Then Hipparinus, Dion's son, and Hipparinus, Dionysius' brother and Dion's nephew through his sister, took control of Syracuse at the instigation of the nobles and began to consider how to govern more honourably. In the meantime Dionysius had gathered an opposing army and was seeking to return to power.

Plato therefore writes to them, encouraging them and directing them to follow the best type of government: a monarchy subject to laws and an aristocracy supported by authority. Such directives can be gathered from various parts of this letter. It is not strange for a man of good talent to choose the government of a republic, especially when necessity requires it; but it is strange for a good citizen to choose to have it when there is complete freedom of choice. It is not the role of a prudent man to involve himself rashly in public affairs, especially when he faces danger with the hope of public protection. In both public and private affairs it is philosophy alone that can discern what is good and just and what is not. The human race will not stop busying itself with evils until philosophers rule or until rulers practise philosophy under God's illuminating power. An upbringing based on pleasure and extravagance corrupts even divine minds. No immoderate man can be prudent. The state in which the citizens are intemperate no power of law can restrain from suffering frequent changes, always for the worse. Violence should never be used against one's country or parents, but care should be taken to keep both of these far from violence. The authority of the ancients and of holy utterances should be preferred to all other opinions. Nothing evil can touch a good man. The soul detached from this body pays the penalty for its wickedness according to the sentence of the divine judge. It is better to suffer the most grievous harm than to inflict it. The grasping and the intemperate are so blind and deaf to matters divine that they themselves cannot see them, they cannot bear to hear of them from others, and if they *do* hear of them they do not grasp them. Irreligion is intermingled with all kinds of sins, and vice versa. Irreligion itself, mingling with sins, is the principal impulse whereby sinners are troubled in this life and tormented in the next.

Later, when he writes of his relationship with Dionysius and of his zeal for philosophy, he shows that no one will make any progress in philosophy unless he be afire with the love of wisdom and thus can bear all hardships for its sake and can scorn all pleasures.

But then, since it is the duty of the wise man to contemplate the divine, he takes this opportunity to show that the divine can never, and should never, be expressed to the general public in writing or by word of mouth: 'can never', because that which is greater cannot be fully comprehended by the mind; and 'should never', because those who are lowest in society would deride things divine as strange phenomena, while those who are a little higher in the social scale, if they were to hear of the divine, might fall into false heresy or become excessively vain and contentious through taking a light view of higher matters.

Nowhere does Plato say that nothing true and assured may be understood about matters divine, but he does say that what is understood of these matters cannot be expressed, and that their intrinsic truth is not understood by that reasoning power which understands everything else.

Indeed, some forms are fully united to bodies, while others are quite separate from bodies: the first are called natural, and the second are called divine. There are also other forms, which are in some way united to bodies and in some way capable of detachment from bodies: these are the rational souls, intermediate between things divine and things natural; they are united to bodies to the extent that they are of necessity detached from things divine, for they cannot be united to forms that are separated from matter, except through their own separation from matter.

168

Now they are separated from matter in two ways especially: by moral purification and by contemplative resolve. The study of philosophy effects both of these ways. Just as a man first dries damp wood in the sunshine before putting it on the fire, thus giving it the opportunity of catching fire, although it is the fire and not the man himself that burns the wood, so the study of philosophy prepares the soul for things divine by moral training and purification, and by contemplative training and resolve takes the mind to things divine and unites it to them, although the study itself does not shape the mind with divine truth, but God Himself, like the fire, fills the mind with the light of His truth, as if the mind were a substance prepared by the good work of philosophy and now brought nigh.

Therefore, when Plato said that divine matters cannot be expressed in writing or by word of mouth, he also meant that they cannot be taught or discovered by that reasoning power which discovers everything else. For in order to perceive other things our own searching prepares and shapes the intellect, but for the perception of things divine even the most purified and perfect search may prepare the intellect but does not shape it, and this is why Plato says that a long acquaintance with things divine is necessary – by which he means long practice of observation – as well as an integration or communion of life – by which he means a purification perfected by moral training.

He adds that the light of truth blazes upon a mind that is finally so disposed: its blaze is immediate and not, as in human fashion, gradual. But where does the blaze originate? It originates in fire, that is, in God, a fire that flashes out sparks. By sparks Plato means Ideas, the models of things in the divine mind. He also means the forms of the Ideas as they take their birth within us; the forms, previously hibernating through inactivity, are aroused by the breath of learning and, flashing forth like rays from the eyes, are illuminated by the Ideas as by rays of starlight.

He adds that such a light is not merely kindled but is created within the soul, that he may show us that the forms are innate to the soul and that such splendour is familiar to us. But lest you should think that the mind is uncertain and agitated in such circumstances, he also adds: 'It – the primal light divinely kindled within the mind – now nourishes itself and then, by its own power, it draws in an abundance of divine rays and fills the mind with restorative joy. This soul nourishes itself – that is, seeking nothing outside itself, it lives content with itself – and the happiness which it experiences inwardly it cannot and does not know how to express, even if it wishes to.'

In this contemplation Plato considers the five levels which you should study in our thorough exposition given in the *Theology*. For he directs the man who is desirous of the truth to begin by hearing the name of a thing; to proceed through sight and the other senses from the trappings of the thing to its definition; to move beyond the definition to the form that is inherent in the mind; and by means of this form to finally reach the Idea which creates forms and things.

He also teaches that an Idea is very different from the four other stages, because an Idea is a substance that is single, motionless, and free from all admixture with an opposite, while the other four – name, incidental manifestation, definition, conceptual form – fall away from the substance, the singularity, the steadfastness, and the purity of the Idea, and this is why they fail to impress the Idea upon us, although they do equip us, as far as they can, to receive the divine impress.

Finally, if a mind that has received the divine impress ever seeks to express the nature of Ideas in words and writings, it will produce nothing but deformed images of the most beauteous of all things. But if it puts its trust in the words of Pythagoras it will not strive to depict Ideas but will rather seek to refine the souls of those who hear and to polish them like writing-tablets on which the divine forms may eventually be depicted by the divine finger.

Such a mind, of course, receiving the heavenly rays, will not make a vain attempt to describe the forms of the rays to the blind. Indeed, if the blind are incurable, it will send them away; but if they are curable, it will seek merely to purify their vision and direct it aloft, that it may understand that its work for any other purpose would be futile.

Discussion by Marsilio of the Eighth Letter,
Written to the Same Relatives and Friends of Dion

I N THE PREVIOUS letter Plato instructed the rulers of Syracuse and turned his attention generally to marriages, precepts, and the actions performed by himself and by Dion.

In this present letter he covers his earlier instructions more briefly, always keeping to a middle course between government by one man and government by the people, but striving most of all to ensure that citizens are reconciled rather than banished and that, as far as is possible, the status of a republic is rightly established without harm to anyone else.

Quite near the beginning he states that men defiled by irreligious wickedness are incurable and that no counsel will profit them. Again, whenever anything needs to be spoken or considered, one should start from God.

In the whole of this letter you will notice what a careful and merciful ruler Plato is, and how hard he works to reconcile souls. He gives his full approval, as he often does, to any government similar to that of Sparta, a government led by the aristocracy, with some permanent form of monarchy and with a touch of democracy.

He condemns slavery in its extreme form, in which everything is subordinate to man's lust. He also rejects all extreme forms of liberty, or licence, in which the government of the state is handed over without any discrimination whatsoever.

He approves of the middle course. Note his golden words: 'Service given to God is well-measured, but that given to men exceeds the measure. Law is the god of temperate men, but lust is the god of the intemperate.'

Discussion by Marsilio of the Ninth Letter

I N THIS LETTER to the philosopher Archytas, who is preoccupied with public affairs, Plato counsels contemplatives not to shirk actions which are honourable and needful; for, he says, actions which are honourable and needful are those that benefit humanity both publicly and privately.

Such actions are honourable because, just as each part of the body lives not for itself but for the other parts and, most importantly, for the whole body, so human beings live for others and, most significantly, for the whole human race.

Such actions are also needful, because unless you live for others you cannot live for yourself, and unless you succour your household and your country, the ship of home and state, being deprived of its helmsman, will pitch and roll, or, if worse men are at the helm, it will founder and eventually be wrecked.

Discussion by Marsilio of the Tenth Letter

PLATO CONFIRMS the views and life of Aristodemus, a friend of Dion and a man of gracious ways, who pursues philosophy first and foremost.

Plato declares that the substance of philosophy is moral virtue, which, he explains, is characterised by love and virtue. He says that man's reflections are either the outer adornments of philosophy or the ways of good living for the attainment of steadfast purity of mind.

After the attainment of this purity, which is divine rather than human and which, rather than being acquired, is imparted from above, there follows contemplation, to which the earlier reflection is directed and which Plato calls a game; but it is the most important direction given by Pythagoras and Socrates.

Now the word which we have translated as 'adornments' means in Greek 'adornments that are shot through with artful vanity and pride', as if Plato were saying, 'Knowledge puffs up; love builds up' or 'Wisdom will not enter a soul that is bent on evil'.

But Plato finds sincerity and wholeness in a soul that is simple and peaceful; trustworthiness in what it says; and steadfastness in its activities and actions.

Discussion by Marsilio of the Eleventh Letter

T O THE REQUEST from the ruler Laodoman about the best type of rule Plato gives his usual counsel: all laws are futile unless the most upright men, through whom the laws live, wield great power in the state and unless there is established within the state a judiciary with plenipotentiary powers which will act as a moral censor in keeping a close watch, through its spies, on the actions of individual citizens, with the constant aim of leading souls to courage and temperance through the daily life of the citizens.

Discussion by Marsilio of the Twelfth Letter

T HE TWELFTH LETTER demonstrates to us Plato's magnanimity and simplicity, for he entrusted to Archytas some of his more recondite commentaries before they were polished.

The theme of the letter is that Archytas, who studied philosophy more in words than in practice, was worthy to receive at this time those things which are most precious. But perhaps the aim was to complete the *Critias* commentary, which was as yet unfinished, and to arrange the *Hermocrates*, which was not yet in its final order.

As for the letter to Dionysius, which ignorant people attach to the commentaries, we have not translated it, because all the learned men say that its words are not Plato's words.

However, it is worth noting in these letters the magnanimity and constancy displayed by our Plato, especially in matters that concerned his friends, and the serious dangers which he braved to protect a friend. We should note, too, the generosity and kindness with which he quite frequently rebuked the tyrant, being more of a stranger to flattery than anyone else but yielding to no one in love and duty, in order that he might be able, as much by his life and character as by his discussions, to help us to live well and happily.

PART THREE

Appendices

Translator's Notes to Part Three

Tarndell hasn't read Hankins

1. Cosimo de' Medici was the Florentine statesman who established a society based on Plato's Academy and who appointed Ficino to lead it. Cosimo directed Ficino to put Plato's Dialogues into Latin and was thus the eminently worthy recipient of this dedication by Ficino of the first ten translations.

2. Various members of the Valori family gave their support to the printing and publication of much of Ficino's work. It was to Niccolò Valori that Ficino dedicated his tenth book of Letters as well as his commentaries on Plato's Dialogues. *Letter of De Vita.*

Introduction by Marsilio Ficino of Florence to the Ten Dialogues of Plato, Translated for Cosimo de' Medici, Father of His Country

n even Field

illippo
for —

WHEN PLATO, the father of philosophers, wrote to Dionysius, Tyrant of the Syracusans, he stated that the nature of power and wisdom was such that they yearn for each other and, through a natural impulse, unite as closely as they are able to. His reason for thinking this is perhaps the fact that the cause of all things is accompanied by the *See* mind, the power of nature is conjoined with order, and the power of *p.150* human skill is accompanied by reason and by an ordered sequence of what needs to be done. *I repeats what said in Pref.*

This is why princes and people in power summon learned men to themselves, and why skilful people, for their part, flock to princes from *to* all directions. Hence arose the close relationship of the wise Simonides *Letter* with Hiero and Pausanias; of Thales of Miletus with Periander of *One* Corinth; of Anaxagoras with Pericles; and of Croesus and Solon with Cyrus. Following these examples, the poets link Creon and Tiresias; Polydus and Minos; Agamemnon and Nestor; Ulysses and Palamedes; and perhaps even Prometheus and Jupiter.

Indeed, Plato prophesied that the human race would not live in happiness until power and wisdom came together, not in two hearts but in one and the same heart, for then the golden age would return once more. He therefore ardently desired to see these two linked together, and he bewailed the fact that this had never happened during his lifetime. But although this was not permitted when he was alive, it was eventually granted after his death: for his spirit, alive in his writings and resonating in the Attic tongue, long ago flew from Byzantium to Cosimo de' Medici in Florence; and in order that Plato might discourse with Cosimo in Latin as well as in Greek, it seemed worthwhile for us to put into Latin some of his enormous Greek output.

We therefore ask you, fortunate Cosimo, to accept twelve Platonic works: ten of Plato's dialogues, and two works by his followers Speusippus and Alcinous. The first dialogue is *Hipparchus,* on the desire for gain. The second is on philosophy, and the third is *Theages,* on wisdom. *Meno,* on virtue, is fourth, followed by the greater *Alcibiades,* on the nature of man, and then the lesser *Alcibiades,* on prayer. The seventh place is taken by *Minos,* on law, and the eighth by *Euthyphro,* on holiness. Then come *Parmenides,* on the One, and finally *Philebus,* on the highest Good.

That the explanatory titles of these dialogues require a sequence of this kind may be gathered particularly from the fact that the desire for the good is innate in everyone. But in their tender years men are deceived by their senses and by opinion, considering the possession of transient things to be beneficial, and so they set about achieving this with all their might and main. This is why *On the desire for gain* is the first book in the sequence. But when men are more mature in years and take some counsel from reason, they begin to love the discovery of matters divine as something beneficial. Now the love of wisdom is philosophy and is given the second place in the sequence. This is followed by *On wisdom,* because through love we seek wisdom before we possess it. *Meno,* on virtue, is next because as soon as the light of wisdom arises, it grants to all the powers and movements of the soul a grace which indeed receives the name of virtue.

Virtue bestows three powers on the soul: the power to return to itself, the power to return to its own cause, and the power to care for whatever is beneath it. Since the soul is by nature the mean between the divine and the corporeal, it becomes endowed with virtue when it preserves its nature and does not mingle with what is lower, but turns towards the higher without abandoning its care for the lower. As the soul returns to itself, we have the greater *Alcibiades,* on the nature of man. As the soul is directed to higher things, we have the lesser *Alcibiades,* on prayer. As it governs the world beneath it, we have *Minos,* on law.

After these three comes *Euthyphro,* on holiness, because it accords with them when the soul, keeping its purity, cares for things human through love, and for things divine through purity. But since the divine light floods the mind which has now been purified by holiness, and since God Himself is discerned by its light, the book on holiness is rightly followed by a discussion on the one principle of all things, and this is why *Parmenides* follows *Euthyphro.* And because our happiness consists in seeing God, it is right that *Philebus*, on man's highest Good, is seen to have been placed after *Parmenides*, on the supreme Good of all nature.

After the ten dialogues of Plato it seemed right to have the work of his follower, Alcinous, who concisely surveys the entire teaching of our Plato. To this I have then added the work of Plato's follower, Speusippus, on the definitions of Plato, so that the essence of Plato's thought might be encompassed by these two short works.

We have also added the *Golden Sayings* of Pythagoras, together with his *Aphorisms*, so that something of the teaching of Pythagoras, on whom Plato modelled himself most of all, might be accessible to Latin speakers.

What has been written here concerns the reason for translating the dialogues, their titles, and their harmonious sequence. But let us now move on to *Hipparchus*, on the desire for gain.

The Preface of Marsilio Ficino of Florence to his Commentaries on Plato, Addressed to Niccolò Valori, a Citizen Endowed with Foresight and Great Worth

WHEN PUBLISHING my books, I always consider at length to whom in particular I should dedicate my labours, but with this publication of the Platonic Commentaries there seems to be no space left for such consideration, since our relationship with the ancient Valori family has become so strong that this family has now quite lawfully appropriated all that is mine.

Indeed, my excellent Niccolò, your forefathers, having now studied philosophy for forty years under Plato, have bestowed the greatest care upon the works of Plato over which we have laboured. Firstly, your father, Bartolomeo Valori, an extremely cultivated man and, as I might say, an ornament of our city, together with his father-in-law, Pietro Pacci, a knight of great renown, was often present at our expositions and discussions on Plato, and he praised them with unstinting enthusiasm. Then your elder brother, Filippo, a truly magnanimous man, following the teaching of Plato in the manner of his father, at great expense drew from the darkness into light the books not only of Plato himself but of all his followers as well, books which we had long ago put into Latin. For this reason he merits the greatest gratitude from the Academy. Meanwhile, your paternal uncle, Francesco, a most upright man, resembling his noble grandfather, Bartolomeo, and equally meriting gratitude from the Republic, ever cherishing us with his dutiful care in all the troubles that fell upon me and mine, for a long time gave us these periods of respite.

Finally, you yourself, continuing the kindness shown by your family towards Plato and Marsilio, relieve me every day from pressing domestic cares, and you assiduously cultivate the Platonic teaching. Now in this teaching, what I strongly approve of is the fact that, above

182

all others, you long ago chose to follow the 'Platonic Theology' before everything else. By your choice of this divine study you demonstrated your discrimination, and by your progress in this divine study you quickly showed your wonderful powers of penetration. But since you have chosen and have profitably pursued the highest of all Platonic teachings, the one which easily embraces the whole, all Platonic teachings are justly indebted to you above all others.

Now these teachings are readily available in our commentaries on Plato. This is why, my excellent Niccolò, I have decided to dedicate these writings to you in particular, as pledges of my love for the Valori family, as memorials of their kindness towards me, and, for posterity, as indisputable evidence of their virtues.

Read them therefore, and live in prosperity, a citizen who is undoubtedly most worthy of long life and everlasting prosperity, if indeed any prosperity, or at least any quietness, however brief, has ever been, or will ever be, enjoyed by citizens who handle the helm of such a storm-tossed Republic.

However, in the present disturbance throughout our Republic and throughout the whole of Italy, and with the calamity which is perhaps about to fall upon us unless God averts it, it is the duty of the prudent to wish to practise philosophy, the duty of the wise to know how to practise philosophy, and the duty of the prosperous to be able to practise philosophy.

INDEX

Euterpe
is the voice of Mercury 58
inspired Ovid 58
Euthydemus 99
prepared to teach the
military art for a fee 74
thinks that no one utters
falsehood 106
Euthydemus 23, 30, 66, 74-80
Euthyphro
his false views on holiness
23
scorned by Socrates 107
Euthyphro 23-4, 30, 180
Eutychia pursuit of the good
76
Evangelist the Evangelist 87

Federico Duke of Urbino 4
flattery inflicts great harm
140-1
Flood
an account of events before
the Flood 148
God washed away the sins of
men with a flood of waters
148
floods 141-2, 145
Florence the Attic tongue
flew to Florence 179
frenzy
divine frenzy is the
illumination of the rational
soul 53
four kinds of divine frenzy
54-5
friends
catch friends with the real
beauty of the soul 32
princes perish from lack of
friends 151
friendship definition 30

Gabriel 22
gain the desire for gain is
praiseworthy 9
geometry is the knowledge
of measuring 35
Giuliano de' Medici 4
God
sent down the divine spirit
of Plato 3
the architect of creation 4
God, fortune, and art govern
all human affairs 56
His providence and care 71
disposes all things sweetly
85
disposes all things according
to number, weight, and
measure 85
His special name composed
of four letters 96
is Himself one 98
fills the purified mind of the
good man with the light of
His wisdom 102

God —*contd*
draws all things to Himself
104
touches all things with His
power and orders them
with His gentle sweetness
104
has entrusted us to the purer
daemons 125
is always present to the wise
and holy man 129
saw that all things were good
136
His boundless wisdom
accompanies His limitless
power 152
His nature and existence 155
beyond all the bounds of our
understanding 157
His perfectly single
substance 159
the author and preserver of
all unity 163
fills the mind with the light
of His truth 169
one should always start from
Him 171
gods
three types 145
the inspiration of local
deities important for the
people 147
golden the celebrated golden
age of Saturn 60
Good
all men strive after the Good
9
the Good is twofold 9
the divine or absolute nature
of the Good 10
all things are related to the
Good 136
Gorgias of Leontini 109
follows popular opinion 110
castigated by Plato 110
Gorgias 21, 23, 66, 73, 80, 85,
109-21, 130, 138, 140
Gospels their teaching 159
government
the best type 167
the type approved by Plato
171
the kind of men required
174
grace is indeed beauty 27
gratitude be grateful to your
native land 143
Greater Hippias 81
Greeks 141
their delicate ears 83
and 'Theos' 96

happiness
three names 76
is founded on wisdom and
justice 115
resides in virtue alone 119

harmony
of mind and speech 91
the need to live in harmony
163
healing by divine words 96
health of body and soul
85-6
Hebrews 22
the wise men among the
Hebrews 95
and the name of Adonai 96
Heraclides 161, 167
Heraclitus 33, 36, 98
says that opposites are
friends 32
says that all things are in
flux 38
says that all things are in
movement 41
Hercules
numbered among the gods
94
conqueror of the earth 94
his words on mounting the
steps to heaven 94
Hermes Trismegistus 13,
19, 22, 23, 24, 157, 159
his *Prayers* 20
on daemons and statues 96,
126
Hermias 163
Hermocrates 148
Hermocrates [an unwritten
dialogue] 143, 175
Hermogenes a disciple of
Parmenides 98, 99
Hesiod 56, 102
says that opposites are
friends 32
inspired by Terpsichore 58
Hiero 179
Hipparchus 9, 156, 157, 180
Hipparchus 9, 181
Hipparinus Dion's son 167
Hipparinus Dionysius'
brother and Dion's nephew
167
Hippias the Sophist 10, 72
though he knew not,
believed that he knew 25
does not know what beauty
is 81
most ignorant and most
incapable 81
boastful, brash, grasping 81
a master unskilled in any of
the arts 81
Hippias 25-9, 30, 66
Hippocrates
a young man very eager to
undergo discipline 66
his view of the soul 86
Hippothales mocked by
Socrates 32
holiness
definition 23
function 24

Only when we get to the Memo is the introduction meaty and not just a series of pious platitudes